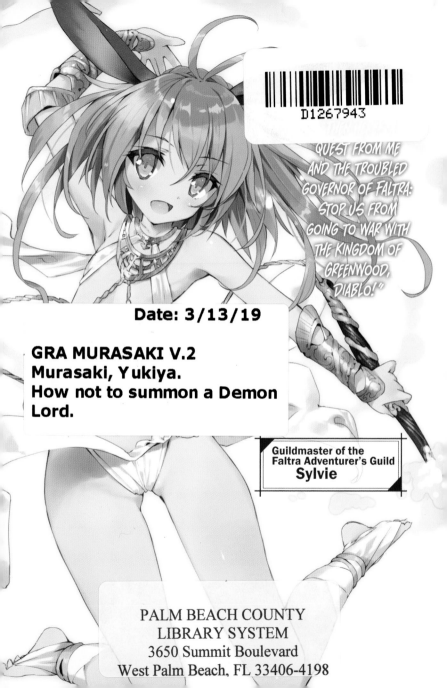

QUEST FROM ME AND THE TROUBLED GOVERNOR OF FALTRA: STOP US FROM GOING TO WAR WITH THE KINGDOM OF GREENWOOD, DIABLO!"

Guildmaster of the Faltra Adventurer's Guild
Sylvie

Sihra's green clothes were turned to foam by the semi-translucent Slime, with her undergarments now exposed. She thought she would die from the shame.

"N-NO... STOP... STOP IT..."

How *NOT* to Summon a Demon Lord

Demon Lord

 VOLUME 2

Yukiya Murasaki
Illust. Takahiro Tsurusaki

How NOT To Summon a Demon Lord: Volume 2
by Yukiya Murasaki

Translated by Garrison Denim
Edited by Kris Swanson

Copyright © 2015 Yukiya Murasaki
Illustrations by Takahiro Tsurusaki

First published in Japan in 2015 by Kodansha Ltd., Tokyo.
Publication rights for this English edition arranged through Kodansha Ltd., Tokyo.

Find more books like this one at www.j-novel.club!

President and Publisher: Samuel Pinansky
Managing Editor: Aimee Zink

ISBN: 978-1-7183-5201-8
Printed in Korea
First Printing: February 2019
10 9 8 7 6 5 4 3 2 1

contents

Cover Art & Illustrations / Takahiro Tsurusaki
Design / AFTERGLOW
Editor / Satoshi Shoji

The Story So Far

In the MMORPG Cross Reverie, Takuma Sakamoto was lauded as the Demon Lord, a being of overwhelming power.

By defeating the 《Demon Lord of the Mind, Enkvaros》, faster than anyone else in the game, he had acquired an extremely rare item: the 《Demon Lord's Ring》. It was one of the ultimate pieces of equipment found in Cross Reverie, able to reflect all types of magic.

Takuma called himself "Diablo," and turned his own personal area in the game into an elaborate dungeon where he acted as its boss. Acting like a Demon Lord, he would entertain any challengers who came to face him—and then destroy them.

And then, one day—

Takuma was summoned to another world that was almost exactly like Cross Reverie.

In front of him were two girls: the Pantherian, Rem, and the Elf, Shera—And then they suddenly kissed him!? They called it an 《Enslavement Ritual》, a ritual magic necessary to control a Summon.

"…I am the one who summoned him. Your magic was a failure."

"You're wrong! He's mine!"

Having performed the summoning magic at the same time, Rem and Shera fought with each other over who really was Diablo's Summoner.

But thanks to the "Demon Lord's Ring" he wore, the magic was reflected. The 《Enslavement Collar》 that should have been put on the Summon to control them was stuck on the girls instead.

Takuma was at a loss of what to do when faced with the two girls arguing. While he may have been a superior player in the game, he had nothing in the way of communicating with other people. After mentally tossing and turning it over in his head, his first words were from the Demon Lord role play he used in the game:

"Cease your pointless squabbling. You are in the presence of Diablo."

After leaving Starfall Tower and testing his magic on the grassy plains, Diablo took the girls and headed towards the nearby city of Faltra.

One of the most important figures in the town, Celes of the Mage's Association, came to visit them at the inn. It seemed Rem was harboring a terrible secret: sealed inside of her body is the soul of the 《Demon Lord Krebskulm》.

Rem was afraid that Diablo would try to distance himself from her when he found out. He told her: "Leave it all to me. No matter what your circumstances may be, I will accept it all."

That night, Diablo was confronted by a man named Galluk. One of Celes's guards, he had a strong elitist attitude. After sending his Summon, Salamander, after Diablo, the self-proclaimed Demon Lord destroyed it with just one blow. As such, he became the target of Galluk's one-sided hatred.

The next day, Diablo and the others headed to the Adventurer's Guild to register themselves as Adventurers. While there was some trouble in determining his level, Diablo managed to receive special permission from the Guildmaster, Sylvie, to become an Adventurer.

Their first quest was a hunt in the fearsome 《Man-Eating Forest》.

Upon their arrival, they found themselves in a trap set by Galluk—an elite squad of Elves had been lying in wait for them, and tried to take Shera back by force. It turned out that Shera was not only a member of the royal family of the Elven Kingdom of Greenwood, but their princess!

The squad of Elves faced Diablo while using the treasures of their kingdom, 《Tempest Arrows》.

Despite this, Diablo easily fended off his assailants.

The difference between their levels was simply too great.

It was then he truly felt the difference between himself, who could respawn even after dying in his game, and for the people of this world, where death was the end.

The following day, when heading out on another quest outside of Faltra—

The Fallen Edelgard spearheaded an invasion with one hundred of her fellow Fallen. At the same time, a powerful Fallen suddenly appeared in the middle of town. Galluk, after having been punished by Celes, had been tempted into assisting the enemy by helping them infiltrate the town.

Rem and Celes were already with each other in the inn when they came under attack from the Fallen. Having been driven into a corner, the two of them were in a hopeless situation.

That was when Diablo appeared. After driving back Edelgard's one hundred Fallen army, he had returned to Faltra via teleportation spell.

Diablo confronted the tenacious Fallen, Gregore, and obliterated the Fallen with his overwhelming magic power. And thus, Celes, Rem, and the town of Faltra were saved.

Prologue

The front lines of the descendants of the Celestials: the Stronghold City of Faltra. Along the western street could be found the 《Peace of Mind Inn - Twilight》.

There was only a solitary window in the stone wall that allowed for light to flow into a dreary room with one large bed.

The time was almost noon.

Three people sat on the bed, while their guest stood in the doorway.

The man in the middle of the bed was a Demon with ominous horns growing out of his head: the Demon Lord, Diablo. On either side of him were girls with enslavement collars around their necks.

One of the girls was the slender Pantherian, Rem Galleu.

The pair of panther ears on her head; the long hair that came down to her waist; and the thin tail that unfurled behind her were all a bewitching black. Normally, Pantherians were leopard-spotted, with black being a rare color for them.

From what could be seen of her thighs, it was easy to see that they were firm and tight.

Her face was young, yet beautiful. Her eyes were slanted like a cat, with her thin mouth showing the strength of her will.

The other girl was the Elf, Shera L. Greenwood.

She had elongated ears known as the particular characteristic that all Elves possessed. Having been called the race closest to the Celestials, they had the beauty to match.

Shera's wavy hair was the same color as melted gold. Her eyes were as cerulean blue as the sky, while her skin was smooth and white.

Usually, she would be wearing a green tunic to help her blend in with the forest...

But right now, she was wearing an outfit consisting of barely anything at all.

It seemed she had prepared this lascivious outfit in order to cheer Diablo up, although this "outfit" was only really a few pieces of cloth wrapped around her.

Normally, Elves were slim and lacking in the "curves" department. Shera, however, possessed a rather robust chest and a sensual body. Even now, it looked like her breasts were going to spill out from what little clothes she was wearing.

Leaning with her back up against the door was the Guildmaster of Faltra's Adventurer's Guild—Sylvie.

It looked like she had the body of a 10-year-old, but her true age was unknown. Grasswalkers like herself would keep their child-like appearance even after reaching maturity. But not only that, she also had the ears and a tail akin to a rabbit's.

Her outfit was similar to what Shera was wearing, with it only covering her chest and the area around her hips. Unlike Shera, however, because Sylvie looked more like a child, it gave off an impression of innocent beauty instead.

The Guildmaster opened her mouth:

"The governor of Faltra received a request from the Elven Kingdom to hand over one Shera L. Greenwood. The deadline is in ten days. If we don't comply by then, they will declare war."

With a smile on her face, Sylvie made the shocking announcement.

—*Declare war!?*

There was a sovereign Elven Kingdom by the name of Greenwood. Shera was the princess there. Due to various circumstances, she had run away from home; but now the Elves were trying to bring her back.

Several days ago, Diablo had fought against an elite squad of Elves trying to do just that. At that time, they were a group of only ten, and by no means could the event have been called a war.

The Guildmaster heaved a sigh.

"Normally, in this situation, you'd hand over Shera, right? We don't want to go to war here. But, there's just one problem with that."

Diablo listened, silently. He had a feeling he knew what she was going to say.

Sylvie pointed a finger at him.

"And that problem is you, Diablo… You're not going to let Shera go, are you?"

"Obviously."

"The governor has to make a decision after receiving a demand like that… That's either to defeat you, Diablo, and steal Shera away; or you don't hand her over, and end up going to war with the Elves."

—*Beat me… or go to war with the Elves!?*

Not good…

Fighting against the governor meant fighting against an army. A huge amount of people would be coming after him.

Back when he put on his Demon Lord act in the game, he had fought against six other people at once.

He had fought against countless monsters—

He had not, however, ever had the experience of fighting against thousands, or tens of thousands, of people. There was no way he had the MP for something like that, either.

Diablo had to give the impression that fighting against him, a Demon Lord, would be disadvantageous to them.

He wanted to avoid an all-out war between Humans and Elves, of course, but first he had to make sure that nobody was coming after him.

All he had to do was skillfully negotiate his way through this…

—*Yeah, that ain't gonna happen.*

Diablo had zilch when it came to communicating with other people. He was using his Demon Lord act as a cover because he couldn't talk well.

He could only stammer out a few "Ah's" and "Um's" if he was acting like his true self.

Though Sylvie had the appearance of a child, she was a Guildmaster with a great number of Adventurers working under her. The governor of Faltra had entrusted her with this task, yet Diablo was not like her. He couldn't even talk to his peers. This was simply too much for him.

It looked like all he had was his Demon Lord role play.

Diablo opened his mouth.

"Heh heh heh… Very well then… I was just getting tired of lying around in bed, anyway. It shall be fitting to have the imperial army as my opponent. I will reduce this country to cinders."

He said it in as low a voice as possible.

In a panic, Sylvie waved her hands in front of her face.

"Wait, wait, hold on now! I'm saying that's *not* an option here! Fighting against you, who took on a whole legion of Fallen by yourself, would be as bad as taking on a whole country… Or maybe even worse."

"Hmph… Looks like you narrowly avoided death."

—By you, I mean me!

While Diablo acted displeased, on the inside he felt nothing but relief.

Sylvie raised her index finger.

"Then here's a quest from me and the troubled governor of Faltra: stop us from going to war with the Kingdom of Greenwood, Diablo!"

—I refuse.

He wanted to say that with every fiber of his being. But, of course, in order to protect Shera, he had no choice but to accept.

The person at the center of this maelstrom of activity timidly cut in.

"U-Um, hey, Diablo… I… I can just, you know… run away by myself again…"

"What?"

Flustered, Shera added:

"B-But! I made it this far running away on my own… And if I'm not around, then there's no reason for Faltra's governor, or for you to have to hand me over to anyone, right?"

"Are you going to be able to escape, by yourself, from the squadrons of Elves after you?"

"Ooh… That's, um… They might catch me… but that's just how it goes. If I fail, then I'm the only one who gets sad… but that's just how it goes…"

She clenched her fists.

Diablo asked her again to confirm.

"'That's just how it goes…' Is that how you truly feel?"

"It is! I mean, I don't want a war! I don't want to see people die! That's why… there's nothing else for me to do!"

He knew what she was trying to say.

She wasn't wrong. If Shera ran away by herself, then the war between Humans and Elves would probably be avoided, and no one would be aiming for Diablo.

But, could she manage to get away?

It would certainly be difficult.

If that's the case, then could he protect Shera while fighting against the Kingdom of Greenwood? That would only be reckless.

What should he do?

If this was when he had first come to this world, he would have refused with no trouble at all. Asking someone to stop a war by themselves was too much for one person to handle. He might have even said "There's nothing I can do about that."

There were no correct choices here.

But he had already given his answer.

That's because, right now—he was the Demon Lord, Diablo!

"Do not underestimate me. There is no feasible way that a Demon Lord would yield to a few soldiers."

Shera opened her eyes wide.

"Huh!? What are you going to do…!?"

"The other day you assented to being property of the Demon Lord, did you not?"

"Y-Yeah. I did say that."

"If you truly meant what you said, then cease this nonsense about running away by yourself. Do you doubt my power?"

"I don't... but... I don't want Humans or Elves to die."

"Hmph. I will not hold myself back against any who dare face me... but, at the very least, I will offer them a warning. Leave everything to me."

There he went again with his Demon Lord role play.

He had just made an exorbitant promise without considering the consequences. His back was covered in a cold sweat, and his mouth almost began to twitch.

Shera teared up.

"...I can... be with you, Diablo?"

"I will not say it again."

"Waaaahhh! Thank you! Thank you, thank you! I was really—!"

Tears in her eyes, she wrapped herself around Diablo.

The feeling of her chest squeezed up against him.

Without thinking, he almost let out a little yelp of surprise, but held fast and resisted the urge. A Demon Lord would not be flustered by having boobs pressed up against him!

Rem let out a sigh.

"...In the first place, because of that enslavement collar on you, it might not even be possible to leave Diablo and do things like run away by yourself."

"Sniff... What do you mean?" Shera asked, wiping her tears.

"...I have never heard of the Enslavement Ritual being reflected before. For that reason, we do not know the exact details about the collars currently wrapped around our necks. However, a Summon cannot normally stray too far from its Summoner."

"Oh, is that right?"

"…In some cases, it is because they are ordered not to leave them."

"But what about when you stayed in town while Diablo and I went to the Bridge of Ulug?"

"…You remember well for a dumb Elf. But for you to run away, you would need to escape to another town, or go even farther away than that. Have you even thought about whether that is possible or not?"

"Don't call me dumb! And no, I haven't really thought about it!"

Rem let out a second sigh.

"…Well, if Diablo says that he will protect you, then I guess there is no need to consider that, anyway."

This was some serious responsibility being laid on him. While seemingly calm and collected on the outside, he was a turmoil of panic on the inside.

—*What do I do? WhatdoIdowhatdoIdowhatdoI*—

Sylvie clapped her hands together.

"Alrighty, everything's decided, then! Whew, glad that's all taken care of. To tell the truth, the Kingdom of Greenwood actually put out a bounty for capturing Shera— Ah, but not through the Adventurer's Guild! We don't make quests out of crimes! It's just a rumor I heard floating around, that's all. So you might have a few 'misguided' Adventurers gunning for you… But that's no problem if Diablo is going to protect you!"

Diablo furrowed his eyebrows.

"The King of Greenwood… Shera's father did that?"

"No, the client was apparently Prince Keera. Sounds like whoever brings her back gets a one billion frith reward. For a commoner, that's enough money for an entire lifetime."

"...What a complete lack of common sense," Rem muttered.

Shera had a horrified expression on her face. Without thinking, Diablo raised his voice.

His rage overtook him.

"He placed a bounty... on his own sister? How could he be any more of an imbecile!"

A black aura suddenly emanated from the entirety of his body.

Rem, Shera, and Sylvie all cried out in shock.

When his feelings had gone out of control after hearing something as ridiculous as a sibling placing a bounty on their sister, it felt like he had consumed a bit of his MP.

Thinking back on it, he felt that his magic was stronger when he took the time to get a clear picture of it in his head.

There may just be a connection between emotions and magic.

—*What would have happened if I was holding Tenma's Staff? I don't think it'd be a good thing if my magic just spontaneously fired off,* thought Diablo.

Because he had been living an idle and lazy life for the past few days, his all-important Tenma's Staff was lying in the corner of the room.

Diablo took a deep breath and calmed himself down.

"Hmph... If there are any Adventurers out there blinded by greed, I will make them regret challenging me."

Sylvie gave a bitter smile.

"Pretty reckless of them, I know. But I'm thinking the Adventurers coming from other towns probably don't know how strong you are, Diablo. I think only the people who saw you fight with the Fallen would believe it."

"Do you not share information amongst each other?"

If something this big had happened in the game, the Wikis and other info exchange sites would be going crazy. Pictures and videos would spread like wildfire, with speculation threads and memes popping up everywhere.

Since there was no internet in this world, he at least thought it would become a topic brought up in small talk at the bars, but it was a complete surprise to hear it wasn't spreading at all.

"There's two reasons for that— The first is that you're an 'Elemental Sorcerer,' right, Diablo? As you know, when you mention 'Sorcerer' in the Kingdom of Lyferia, everyone is going to think of 'Summoners.' Elemental magic is thought to be weak, after all," Sylvie explained.

In Cross Reverie—the MMORPG he used to play that was remarkably similar to this world—when you thought of Sorcerers, you thought of Elemental Sorcerers.

The reason was simple: it was because they were the most powerful class.

By choosing skills that would enhance their elemental magic, they would be considered a success once they made one of the six elemental trees into a weapon of mass destruction for themselves.

That's why Summoners in the game were seen as a fool's class. They tried their best to bring out their Summons, but the Summons were still weaker than a Warrior of the same level.

Their stats were about the same, but Summons only possessed one special skill. A Warrior, who possessed a wide variety of skills, held an overwhelming advantage.

The only real advantage that could be said for the Summoner would be that even if their Summon was defeated, they would take none of the damage dealt to them.

Summoners in Cross Reverie were scorned as a weak class that was "for n00bs;" "for people lacking in the information (and brain) department;" it was a class that was "cool, but impractical."

However, this world was different.

In the Kingdom of Lyferia, at the very least, Elemental Sorcerers were weak, while Summoners were strong—

And he knew the reason why.

Unlike the game, where you could be brought back to life if you ran out of HP, death in this world meant it was all over.

Most Adventurers here did not chase after rare items or try to raise their levels; they were satisfied to live their lives being strong enough to go about on a day-by-day basis. They did not seek to train themselves up by risking their lives fighting powerful enemies; they were merely thinking about not dying while trying to save up enough money to support themselves.

The same could be said of the monsters.

They didn't try to recklessly attack you like in the game. When they saw an opponent they knew they did not stand a chance against, they possessed the cowardice to run away, and were weak because of that.

As a result, it wasn't that Summoners were strong—it was that everything around them was weak. That's why Summons were so useful here.

The Summoner staying safe was also a great advantage for themselves.

In the face of all these values, of course the Adventurers of this world wouldn't believe it if someone told them there was a "strong Elemental Sorcerer out there."

They might laugh and brush it off, thinking it was a lie. At best, they might think that he was strong "for an Elemental Sorcerer."

As a gamer, having the class he poured so much time and effort into be mocked and sneered at like this was a feeling of mortification he would not forget.

But, he had to put those feelings aside and accept it: in this world, Elemental Sorcerers were thought to be weak.

"Hmph... Regarding me as if I was the same as the other Elemental Sorcerers of this world..."

"Well, of course that'd happen. Your power kind of defies imagination, you know. There's also another reason— It's because I'm keeping people quiet about it."

"Oh hoh?"

"I thought it might have been unnecessary myself, but it seems like you all have some stuff going on, right? That's why I thought it might be better for you to not stand out so much, though I don't know the particulars of what you're going through."

—*Did she really just guess that, or is she hiding the fact that she knows something?*

At the very least, it seemed she was aware of Shera's background. Never mind that the person herself kept letting that information slip to almost everyone she met, despite her saying she wanted to keep it a secret...

Diablo, however, was more interested in whether or not Sylvie knew about Rem's circumstances.

"You say that you don't know the particulars... But how much *do* you know?"

"Ahaha… All I know is that it just kinda seems like there's something going on with you guys, honest. Shera being the princess of the Kingdom of Greenwood has been a pretty big topic of discussion here ever since she came to town. And since Rem here always seems to keep her distance from other people, I just feel like she's got some of her own problems she's dealing with… And, well, it's because I've seen these kinds of things before."

It was when Sylvie said stuff like this Diablo felt that she was older than him, despite her childish appearance.

—Well, she is the Guildmaster, after all.

She must have the appropriate experience for the job.

Standing beside Diablo, Rem lowered her head.

"…We are very grateful for your concern."

"It's fine, really. If I can help you with anything, make sure and let me know. I think of all the Adventurers in Faltra as my friends."

"…Thank you very much."

—What a masterpiece of communication that was.

Sylvie offered a proposal:

"Well, on that note, I'm not going to pry into whatever those circumstances may be, so how about coming to stay with me? The Adventurer's Guild has rooms you can stay in for times like these. I think it would be much safer than here. If I asked him, I think the governor would prepare a room for you at his place, but I think it'd be a lot more comfortable for you to come hang out with me."

It was an enticing plan. But was it all right for him to agree to this so easily? It seemed like Sylvie was the kind of person he could trust…

—But can I really?

Diablo couldn't come to a decision. He felt sorry for doubting her good intentions…

But Diablo was severely lacking in his people skills. If he could just be honest and say, "Let's get along," then he wouldn't be the eternal solo player that he was.

He was bad at closing the distance between himself and others.

He would put his trust in them, get to know them better… But then they turned out not to be as devoted as he thought they were, and he would get betrayed.

If he was worried about the distance between them, then it was easier not to get close in the first place.

He would figure out how to avoid this war by himself. He didn't know how, but he would just figure it out along the way.

This was the calm before the storm—and that storm was war.

This hadn't yet turned into a quest to "Stop the enemy soldiers in their tracks." He had to do his best to prevent that from happening.

—*What should I do here?*

First, I need to get some information.

The basic strategy for any quest was to gather information. This world wasn't a game, but he could only approach it as if it were.

Diablo opened his mouth to make a specific request.

"I am not partial to being indebted to other people. More than that, I want—"

He was interrupted by a thunderous crash.

†

The stone wall behind him collapsed.

The walls of the inn were made from stones of various sizes stacked on top of each other and held together with lime mortar. It wasn't like they were flimsy, but they were no castle walls, that's for sure.

It could probably be broken by using magic or a large-sized weapon.

—*But who destroyed it?*

Sylvie jumped away from the doorway, yelling.

"They're coming from the door, too!"

She landed next to the bed, at Diablo's side.

Immediately after, the door to the room was smashed open.

Diablo ran his eyes over his surroundings to get a grasp on the situation.

Four people had entered the room: Adventurers, fully armed.

Three of them came from the hallway. One of them was a Dwarven Warrior, who carried a war axe.

The characteristics of a male Dwarf were their short and stout stature, burly muscles, and a beard that completely hid their mouths and necks. They were slow on foot, and weren't suited for magic; but they excelled when it came to brute strength and tenacity. They were naturally gifted with the talents needed for the Warrior class.

Everything about this assailant truly screamed "Dwarf."

Following the Dwarf were two gloomy-eyed Grasswalker Warriors in light armor.

Just like Sylvie, they had the ears and tails of a rabbit, and a childlike exterior. The expression in their eyes, however, was sharp.

These two Grasswalkers had the exact same face. It wasn't that they just looked similar because they were the same race, it was like they were mirror-reflections of each other.

—*Twins?*

They were armed with daggers, and stared onwards with dark, stagnant eyes.

The one who had entered through the destroyed wall was a Pantherian fighter, equipped with metal claws on both hands.

As their name would suggest, Pantherians were a race who bore ears and tails like that of a panther, housed atop flexible, lithe bodies. Because of their superior agility and physical strength, they excelled in close combat.

Diablo and the others gathered around the bed in the center of the room.

It wasn't that wide a space, and they were soon surrounded on all sides.

—These guys are supposed to be Adventurers!?

"…Did you not notice this!? You seem like you would be able to detect an attack like this before it happened!" Rem asked Shera, accusingly.

Shera had easily sensed an elite squad of Elves who had been concealing themselves in the forest before. She had also inferred where the battle with the Fallen in town had taken place.

She possessed a very keen sense of perception.

For her not to have noticed this attack coming… Were their opponents just that exceptional? Or was there another reason?

Shera puffed out her cheeks.

"There are too many people in this town, so I can't tell!"

—So that's what it was.

There were a great number of people in this town. Trying to find those who were coming closer to them with malicious intent was probably harder than finding Elves in the forest for her.

In any case, they were thrust into a sudden fight.

—*If possible, it would be great if I could get them to back off by threatening them.*

Diablo spoke in a fearsome voice:

"For you fools to appear before me... I assume you no longer wish to live."

The two Grasswalker twins whispered to each other.

"He's asking if we don't want to live anymore, big brother."

"He did indeed ask us if we didn't want to live, little brother."

"Should we answer?"

"No, we will not. Our target isn't the Demon."

"Understood, big brother— There she is. It's the Elf."

"Yes, it's that Elf."

Covering her immodest outfit with a blanket, Shera froze.

"M-Me!? I don't even know who you are!"

Dumbfounded, Rem once again let out a sigh.

"...Sylvie *just* explained this to us. These people are Adventurers... No, they are mere criminals after the bounty being offered by the Prince of Greenwood for your capture."

Diablo ground his teeth together.

—*Damn! I left Tenma's Staff in the corner of the room!*

In Cross Reverie, you needed to carry a staff until you reached level 30 or else you wouldn't be able to use elemental magic. After you passed that level, then you could use magic regardless of your equipment loadout.

Diablo was level 150, so he could conjure magic without any problems, but having his staff made it easier to aim and control the power of his spells.

Not only that, but Tenma's Staff would raise the user's INT stat, and also shorten the cast time for magic.

His equipment at the moment consisted of the 《Distorted Crown》, an item with an HP regeneration effect that made him look like he had twisted devil horns growing out of his head; and the 《Demon Lord's Ring》, a super rare item that would reflect any spell thrown at the wearer.

Right now, he wasn't wearing the 《Curtain of Dark Clouds》, his cape that protected him from bad status effects and instant death; or the 《Ebony Abyss》, a pitch-black outfit that reduced physical damage and boosted the wearer's stats.

He had let his guard down, which is why he was currently in this desperate situation.

—But I have to protect Shera!

Rem reached into one of the pockets of her leather belt to pull out a crystal. If she threw it, she would be able to use a Summon.

"…Come forth! Shadow—"

"Who-ho-hoh there!"

The Dwarf Warrior rushed in, swinging his war axe.

—He's faster than I thought. Is he about level 20?

Diablo pulled Rem towards himself.

"Kyahh!?"

The enemy's assault ended with him swiping at thin air.

Rem's concentration interrupted, she hadn't been able to call her Summon.

Rem looked up at Diablo.

"Th-Thank you…"

"Don't push yourself. You can leave it to me."

The Dwarf licked his lips.

"Magic's pretty dern inconvenient, ain't it? If ya git beaten afore you can use it, den dere's no point to it, is dere!"

They were in the middle of a small room, already within range for close-quarters combat.

Most likely, these guys were thinking that they would be able to react before Diablo could do anything.

—*These guys are all slow compared to me,* Diablo thought to himself.

With his high AGI stat, it seemed like he could fire off three spells in the time it would take the Dwarf to move once.

But, if Diablo used some kind of offensive magic against him, the Dwarf might end up dead.

There was also the option to try and miss on purpose, aiming for the floor or the wall, or something, but he was already too close.

Never mind himself, but he might end up hurting Rem and the others at this rate.

Since a portion of the wall was already knocked out, if things went any further it was possible that the roof could come down on them, too.

—*Can I win barehanded like this?*

He didn't have much experience when it came to this. If it was just a one-on-four fight, then he might be able to do it.

But while he was fighting, what if they nabbed Shera? What if Rem was cut down?

—*And now that I think about it, where's Sylvie?*

She should have jumped to his side after the door had been busted down.

He remembered that much, but after he had pulled Rem out of the way of that attack to protect her, Diablo had suddenly lost sight of Sylvie.

Suddenly, Sylvie's voice rang out in the room.

"《Ivy Bind》!"

A burst of magical light surged around where the Dwarf stood. Thick vines grew and stretched out from the floor.

"—Hell? What in tarnation is this!?"

The Dwarf yelled out in surprise, but it was already too late.

The vines rapidly wrapped themselves around the Dwarf, restraining him.

At some point, Sylvie had moved to one of the corners of the room. It was a position where she was out of reach of the Grasswalker twins and the Pantherian's attacks.

Though she should have been right next to him, that was one incredible Stealth skill she had used.

As would be expected of the Guildmaster, she was truly knowledgeable about fighting multiple opponents at once.

This was a powerful magic that was capable of inflicting the "Bind" status on an opponent, and sealed their movement for a limited period of time.

Diablo was unable to use it.

Ivy Bind was a support spell. It only stopped an opponent from moving, and couldn't actually defeat them. When used with a group of other people, that's when its effects really shined, but there was little point in using it as a solo player.

Considering Diablo's magic power, it was more damage efficient for him to fire off some offensive magic instead of using a roundabout spell like that.

—After all, there wasn't a time back in the game where I had to worry about not killing my opponents.

Sylvie yelled out in a sharp voice.

"You aren't Adventurers from Faltra, are you! Where did you come from!?"

The two Grasswalkers started whispering again.

"That's Faltra's Guildmaster, big brother."

"That's the Guildmaster all right, little brother."

"That was unexpected, wasn't it."

"Yeah, completely unexpected."

They spoke in the exact same voice, tone and all. It was creepy, to say the least.

The twins stared at each other.

"Should we keep going, big brother?"

"No, we're at a disadvantage, little brother."

"Then should we leave him behind?"

"No, we won't leave him yet."

"Understood, big brother. If that's the case—"

One of the Grasswalkers pulled something out of the pouch around his waist.

—*Is he planning on using an item!?*

The small tube he brought out began to shine brightly.

His vision was enveloped in a dazzling white light.

"Ngh!"

Diablo grunted.

He was completely blinded.

—*That was a flash bomb!*

These items could be created using a Crafting skill, and would inflict the "Blind" status to everything within a fixed area.

Any player who was blinded received a penalty to their evasion, accuracy, and movement.

To cure it, you needed to either possess some kind of healing magic, use an item, or wait until the effects wore off.

Though the effects of a flash bomb were short lived, it had a high chance of success. That's why it was a popular item that almost all Adventurers had ended up relying on at least once in their careers.

But even without the Curtain of Dark Clouds, Diablo had a much higher resistance than the other Adventurers here, so it did not affect him much.

From his narrowed field of vision, he saw the two Grasswalkers throwing the Dwarf over their shoulders.

Ivy Bind would prevent the target from moving. So even in the game, other members of the party would be able to move freely.

—*But you can carry a bound party member!? Is that even possible!?*

There was no command to "Carry" someone in the game.

For just an instant, Diablo was struck by a sense of surprise.

Carrying the Dwarf on their shoulders, the Grasswalkers managed to move surprisingly quick as they escaped into the hallway.

The Pantherian also left through the hole they had made in the wall.

—*Should I chase after them and leave Shera here?*

Even if he caught them, what kind of information would he get? There probably wasn't much point to doing that.

There was also no way for Diablo to incapacitate them without killing them.

As he hesitated about what to do, he eventually lost sight of their attackers.

†

Diablo looked around the now quiet room.

The door was broken. It had come off its hinges and was lying on the floor.

The wall behind the bed in the center of the room was crumbling away, window and all.

—*This is the second floor, so how the hell did they do that? I can't believe they used their power as Adventurers for something this stupid...*

Fragments of the stones that lined the wall, the lime mortar that held it together, red clay, and grains of sand all littered the floor. The place looked like an abandoned building.

—*This just looks awful.*

It was maddening that they had managed to get away, but he did applaud their judgment in doing so, however.

They probably weren't expecting Sylvie the Guildmaster to be here, let alone being inflicted with the "Bind" status.

From what he experienced in the game, being faced with an unforeseen dilemma was related to the party often being wiped out. While you worried about how to deal with the situation, you lost your chance to escape.

These people had come to a decision quickly. They deserved to be praised for at least that much.

Their choice was on the mark as well.

Perhaps because their lives were on the line, they were fast to make a retreat, and were strongly fixated on avoiding being wiped out.

—In this world, death doesn't mean you just come back to life at a spawn point after losing some experience points. Death actually means death here.

The more he thought about it, the harder it was to use his most powerful magic.

Even if he hadn't heard Shera's plea earlier, Diablo didn't want to kill anyone.

But he wasn't going to pretend that he was some kind of saint that wouldn't even harm a fly. If someone was hostile to him, then there might be times where he took their life. To put it bluntly, his own life was much more important than the life of some stranger.

If it was to save someone he actually knew, he probably would end up forsaking a life he didn't even know.

—But I think there's a difference between "someone dying because of an unavoidable battle" and "straight up killing someone."

At the very least, I want to make an effort to try and go easy on people.

As he thought that, it seemed Rem and Shera had finally regained their sight. Normally, the effects of a flash bomb only lasted about ten seconds.

For Diablo, though, it only dazed him a little. Sylvie also seemed to be relatively unaffected.

Looking around the room, Rem breathed a sigh.

"…So, they escaped… I'm sorry, it seems I held you back."

"What are you saying? They came to the realization that their greed was unmerited and ran off, that's all. They are just like insects fearing for their lives as they escape through the window; there is no need for you to worry yourself about it."

Rem gave a timid nod.

Then, she turned her gaze towards Sylvie.

"…Thank you for saving us."

"Well, I was thinking about leaving it all to Diablo, since he was here. But I thought if I didn't do something, you might think that I was the one who planned the attack."

Shera called out as well.

"Thanks for protecting us! I'm really grateful, too!"

Sylvie stuck out her nonexistent chest.

"Heh heh heh… I *am* a Guildmaster, after all. I know a thing or two about holding down rowdy punks. In fact, you could almost call me an expert in it!"

—*I see, so she trained herself in Bind magic.*

She was what you would call a "Support Sorcerer."

In Cross Reverie, they were greatly coveted when in a party, but were a pain to play solo, so they were extremely rare.

They were a class more valuable than Healer Sorcerers.

Whenever he laid eyes on a strong enemy, the first thing that popped into Diablo's head was how he would fight it.

Sylvie was a Grasswalker. By nature, she was a master of Stealth skills, and possessed superior AGI stats. She could move around without being detected, and even if she was, she could nimbly dodge anything thrown at her. Covering for her flimsy defense likely was when she would unleash her Bind magic.

Warriors would be more affected by "Bind", but could a Sorcerer like Diablo have his magic sealed away by "Silence?"

—*I have equipment that prevents negative status effects, so I guess there's no problem there.*

Using support magic showed how skilled the user was as a player.

Though they were difficult to use, when in the hands of a skilled player, they were an extremely dangerous threat.

Support Sorcerers weren't just geared towards playing with a party, they could *only* be used in a party. It felt like it was a class only for normies who could actually communicate with other people.

He knew that it would never be suited for him, and there was nothing he could do about it.

—I may be a bit prejudiced towards them, but I always thought of them as "pure on the outside, black on the inside."

There shouldn't be any problems one-on-one, but he had to make sure to take great care if he ever fought Sylvie. He would be careful to make sure that it wouldn't come to that, though.

As Diablo stared at Sylvie, she adorably tilted her head to the side.

"What's up?"

He had to avert his eyes from this sudden surprise attack.

—No! A Demon Lord does not blush or avert his eyes when a girl (is what she looks like, she's probably an adult) does something really cute!

With a "Hmph", Diablo haughtily threw has head back.

"If you had not stepped in, my magic would have annihilated them from this world."

"Ahaha, now that sounds scary… You sure managed to hold yourself back, didn't you, Diablo. I think it was a good decision not to kill them."

"I was not holding myself back. I saw what you were trying to do, so I simply decided to watch."

—That's a big fat lie.

He had lost sight of Sylvie.

There was a big difference between Sneak skills here and in the game.

Not only that, but he wasn't used to having allies around, either.

Sylvie shrugged her shoulders.

"Though I think it would count as justified self-defense, even if you did end up killing them... Killing someone in the middle of town using magic would definitely lead to some kind of investigation. While that's going on, you wouldn't be able to protect Shera. There wouldn't be any point in an acquittal, you know?"

"I have no intent to cooperate in any kind of investigation."

"Hmm, but you would be going up against soldiers under the direct supervision of the governor, or even the royal capital. If you try to resist, you'd just turn into a wanted man. It wouldn't just be Faltra; you wouldn't be able to stay anywhere in the entire Kingdom of Lyferia. Even if you were okay with a vagabond lifestyle and not being able to use inns or shops, I'd think it would be pretty rough on Rem and Shera."

He couldn't deny that.

—So if I ended up killing them, it'd be treated like I PK'd someone.

There was a PK (player kill) system in Cross Reverie.

Whether it was in the field or in a town, if you killed a player (even if it was an accident on your part) you would be hunted down like a criminal in the game.

Your name would be displayed in red, and if you tried to enter a town some crazy strong knights would appear who could cut you down in one slash. A bounty could be placed on your head by the country, and you would be in a position where other players would aim for you as well. It was almost the same as becoming one of the monsters in the game.

It seemed you would be treated the same in this world as well.

Diablo had fought against a great number of people in battles, but he had never PK'd someone before.

There was also a PvP system implemented into the game.

Players could face off with each other within dungeons built in their own personal spaces.

It was normally one-on-one, but as long as there was a mutual agreement for it, it could even turn into one-on-six fights.

In any case, on top of it being a fight that both sides agreed to, there was no chance of death for the losers. All that would happen was their money and goods being taken from them.

If you won, your battle record would improve, and the amount of EXP you received would be greatly increased.

Putting PvP aside for the moment.

—*Not using magic on those guys might have actually been a really nice move on my part!*

Now that he knew he had successfully made it past a particularly extreme choice, his pulse started to beat faster.

But a Demon Lord wouldn't let something like this make his heart rate go up, so he kept pretending like he didn't care in the slightest.

"Hmph… So you're saying that others like the ones who just attacked will come after us as well."

"Probably, yeah. That's why I suggested preparing a room for you all at the Adventurer's Guild—But it seemed like you were trying to say something earlier, right, Diablo?"

—*Oh yeah, that's right.*

He had completely lost his train of thought when their assailants busted in.

An essential to clearing any quest was to first gather information. And as of now, the person who seemed like they had the most information that he could talk to would be…

"Sylvie. I'm going to speak with the governor."

"Mmm… I see…"

It seemed she had anticipated what Diablo was going to ask for.

It was only natural for someone accustomed to taking on quests to think as such.

"If you say you won't take us, however, then that means I will go on my own."

"Sigh... I know that's what you want and all... But I'm a little nervous about it. You're not very good at being polite with people, you know?"

—*I'm polite to everyone, even to people working at convenience stores and stuff!*

...But a Demon Lord would never say that.

That especially went for now, since Diablo had to make everyone think that fighting against Diablo would be worse than going to war with the Kingdom of Greenwood.

There was no way he could start acting prim and proper now.

—*But it's a problem if I can't get any information... I guess there's no way around it then.*

"Hmph... I was only thinking of meeting him on a whim... But if you're going to refuse me, then that makes things interesting. I will burn that mansion to the ground. If I do, I'm sure the governor is will come running out... Heh heh heh..."

"Whoa there, hold it! Time out! I didn't refuse anything! Ah, geez... I'm not that good dealing with the governor either... But I'll take you there. You should be able to see him."

On the inside, Diablo felt relieved.

If he was just able to meet with this person, he would be able to get all the information he wanted, since this was a matter of the governor not wanting to go to war.

Hiding how he truly felt, Diablo gave a composed nod of assent.

"I shall allow it. Lead us there."

Rem brushed the dust off her clothes.

"...I will be coming with you, of course."

"I-I'm coming, too!"

As Shera threw the blanket off of herself, her almost naked body was once again exposed to the world.

Rem scowled at her.

"...Go get changed, stupid Shera."

"Huh!? E-Even I wouldn't think about going to the governor's mansion like this!"

"...Never mind the mansion, going outside in that is not OK at all."

The Central District—

Faltra was a stronghold city, fortified on all sides by high and sturdy rampart walls. If you were to look down on it from above, it would be shaped like an octagon, with towers on each one of its eight points.

Each one of those towers was part of a large-scale ritual magic designed to repel monsters and the Fallen. They functioned through the use of magic power—supplied by Celes Baudelaire, the head of the Mage's Association—as a source of energy.

On the other side of the walls were rows of buildings lined up next to each other, and a thoroughfare that connected the east and west sides of the town. It was large enough for an entire army to pass through.

In the center of town could be found another wall. Though not to the extent of the outer walls of the city, it was still extremely solid. This wall surrounded the mansions of the governor, aristocrats, and other exceedingly affluent people who lived within the Central District.

Rather than being there to serve some kind of purpose in case of war, the main intent of this wall was to prevent crime from within.

The thick stone walls were about three stories high. There were only four gates, one located at each of the cardinal points.

All those who had come and gone were under strict surveillance, with multiple halberd-toting guards lined up at each gate. These people were not soldiers, but knights who came under the direct supervision of the governor himself.

Diablo stayed next to Sylvie as he walked. Behind them were Rem and Shera, with Shera wearing her usual green tunic.

Horse-drawn carts passed here frequently through the stone-paved main road.

Along the way, Sylvie began to talk about the governor, explaining that it was best for them all to know the information she held.

Diablo feigned his disinterest in the topic while listening intently to every word.

"Let's see... Before I get to the governor, I'm gonna talk a bit about the town of Faltra itself, and just how important it is, OK? As you already know, this is the front line for the descendants of the Celestials. To the east lies the territories of the Kingdom of Lyferia, where countless people are living. There are plenty of large towns there, with several of them lacking the walls or the soldiers needed to protect themselves from monsters or the Fallen. Basically, if they come under attack from an enemy army, things are not going to go well for them. And to the west of Faltra lies the domain of the Demon Lord."

"...The *former* domain of the Demon Lord, correct?" Rem added.

Sylvie nodded.

"Yup. It may not really feel that way with all the monster and Fallen activity as of late, but it's the former domain of the Fallen. In year 124 of the Lyferian Kingdom calendar, the Demon Lord appeared and made everything to the west of here his territory.

Then, in the year 135, he was defeated thanks to the efforts of some unknown stranger… Or that's what they say, at least. That was the Demon Lord of the Mind, Enkvaros…"

A name Diablo was all-too familiar with.

"Oh yeah, I was the first to defea—"

Before he could say more, he covered his mouth.

—That's right, I only beat him in the game… But the guy here has the same name as the Demon Lord in Cross Reverie!?

Diablo had been the first to beat the Demon Lord Enkvaros before any other player, granting him the Demon Lord's Ring.

He thought back—

Enkvaros possessed the ability of Magic Reflection. Because of that, many of the other players challenged him by making parties focused around the Warrior class. Warriors had low magic resistance, however, and were prone to the effects of spells like 《Confuse》 or 《Sleep》, which could prove fatal for them.

Diablo's specialty was playing solo, so negative status effects were just about the same as instant death to him. That's why he had an abundance of countermeasures for exactly that kind of situation.

Not only that, but he had fortunately learned spells that would deal physical damage for when he had to go up against monsters or opponents who resisted normal magic.

Back in the early days of the game, when there wasn't a lot of information available, the reason he had been able to take down Enkvaros on his first try was sheer luck…and all the time he had spent forging his skills as a player, too.

That was back in the real world, two years ago.

"Now that I think about it, I never confirmed it myself. What year is it now? And how long ago was the Demon Lord Enkvaros defeated?"

"Right now it's year 164 on the Lyferian calendar, so it's been about 30 years since the Demon Lord disappeared."

"I see."

—*Could it be something like time in this world goes ten times faster than time in my world? …No, that would be strange. If I had defeated the Demon Lord 30 years ago in this world's time, then that would mean "Diablo" would have been in this world as well.*

Should I think of this Demon Lord as a separate entity from the game, even though they share the same name?

In the first place, a majority of the players in Cross Reverie had beaten Enkvaros as part of the story quests.

—*That would mean there were millions of Demon Lords then, right?*

According to the game's staff, Cross Reverie had a total of over three million players across the country.

Sylvie continued:

"Well, anyways, the Demon Lord of the Mind, Enkvaros, was said to have been defeated by someone, and both monsters and the Fallen stopped showing up in the former Demon Lord's domain. But… over the past few years, several Fallen have appeared. I mean, just the other day there were a hundred of them, right? There are even rumors spreading around where people are wondering if the Demon Lord has already been resurrected."

"You don't know?"

"It's enough that the seers of the Royal Capital are saying, 'The resurrection is near.' I think the Fallen are working to finish the process they started of reviving the Demon Lord."

Shera had said something similar before as well.

Rem pressed a hand against her chest.

Diablo nodded.

"I do not think he is resurrected as of yet. When I fought Edelgard, the Fallen who had gathered the army of one hundred Fallen, she had said her mission was to 'save the Demon Lord.'"

"What...!? If that's true, that would be some incredible information!"

"Those *are* the words of a Fallen, however."

"Y-Yeah. But I'm still going to pass this along to my contact in the Royal Capital, just in case."

"Do as you like. Putting that aside, weren't you going to talk about the governor?"

"Ah, my bad... Anyways, even if it's the former territory of the Demon Lord, it's just as dangerous as when the Demon Lord was still in this world. When he is resurrected, I'm sure that the presence of monsters will go up as well. The Stronghold City of Faltra is here as the front lines to hold both monsters and Fallen at bay, as well as to protect the territories of all the other races."

If this town were to fall, it was said that half of the Kingdom of Lyferia would come under attack by the Fallen. There was never an event where things got that bad in the game; but if something like that were to happen in this world, who knows what would happen.

What he knew for sure, though, was that an immeasurable amount of people would die.

"...So the person in charge of this all-important location is the governor here."

"That's right, the governor of Faltra. He's a really amazing person; to put it bluntly, he's a hero."

"A hero?" Shera tilted her head.

"Thirty years ago, back when the Demon Lord was still around, he fought on the front lines, slaughtering all kinds of Fallen."

"Wooow. He sounds sooo amazing."

"Ahaha… That doesn't sound too sincere, Shera."

"I mean, Diablo's won against the Fallen, too, you know?"

"Yeah, that's definitely a feat that should go down in history. In fact, it's something so abnormal that no one would believe you if you told them."

Since Shera compared the governor to Diablo, Sylvie seemed to be struggling a little to find the right words.

—*Looking at it from another angle, that means he's so strong that he can't be compared to anyone else.*

"What level would this governor be?" Diablo inquired.

In this world, all the Adventurers around Faltra were about level 20 or so. The outliers would be Rem, who was famous here, sitting around level 40; and the person said to be the strongest Warrior in town, at level 50.

The area around Faltra back in the game was set to be around level 60. Compared to that, everyone's levels were unbelievably low. This was apparently because the people here were avoiding anything dangerous since their lives were on the line. One of the main causes for this was due to there being no Demon Lord present for the past 30 years, and everything was peaceful.

How strong would the governor be, having fought and experienced countless battles with his life on the line?

Sylvie folded her arms.

"Hmm… He's strong, I know that for sure. But I've never tried determining his level… He's not an Adventurer, after all. There might be a record of it in the Royal Capital, but he isn't the kind of person you can just casually ask for such a thing."

"It seems like he's fairly hard to talk with."

"Hmph."

Though Diablo pretended like he didn't care, his unease only grew.

The very essence of his severe lack of communication skills laid in his ability to put others in a bad mood, all just by doing things he hadn't expected to do. And if that person was stern, then that meant there were a lot more chances for Diablo to make them mad.

He just couldn't imagine a future with the two of them getting along.

—*Am I going to be all right doing my Demon Lord role play here? …No, it's already too late to stop doing it now.*

If he didn't make a character for himself like this, he wouldn't be able to talk in front of such important people. If he was his normal self, then he would probably hole himself up in his room; just running away from things and giving up.

—*I can't believe it myself… Me, actually going to meet the leader of the town. The reason I make this character for myself is because it makes this feel more like a game to me. That's why I'm able to make this work, somehow.*

He started to see the stone walls that encircled the Central District.

In the middle of the lofty walls was an imposing gate. A great number of guards were observing the travelers who passed by. As she started jogging towards the guards, Sylvie told Diablo and the girls to wait so she could get permission for them to pass through. She entered a small hut to the side of the wall, most likely to complete whatever process was needed for passage.

Diablo and the others stared at the gate while they waited. As they did, one of the guards in front of the gate started to approach them. His armor made loud clanking sounds with each step he took.

"Hey! The Demon over there!"

His face completely covered by his helmet, the guard called out in a menacing voice.

On the inside, Diablo was shaken up.

—*Is he talking about me!?*

He had been called out by one of the guards back at the Bridge of Ulug because they thought he looked suspicious, too. Back then, he had made it through peacefully... Kind of. At the very least, he had been able to pass without much trouble. It should be all right this time as well.

"What is it, you whelp? For you to approach me, Diablo... I trust you have prepared yourself for doing such a thing."

He couldn't tell if the guard's face changed expressions underneath the helmet.

—*The insignia of the city is imprinted on his armor's chest plate... So this is what a knight who works directly under the governor looks like. Seems like he's got plenty of fight in him.*

The guard was not intimidated.

"There's no way I could overlook someone as suspicious as you!"

The guard pointed the end of his halberd at Diablo's head. There, Diablo had equipped his "Distorted Crown," a piece of armor that granted him automatic health regeneration abilities. He hadn't paid much attention to the description in the game, but it said it was an item that "gives the wearer a more fiendish appearance when worn." More specifically, it made it seem like demon horns were growing out of your head.

It was perfect for doing his Demon Lord role play, but...

—*These horns make everyone really suspicious of me, don't they...*

But to Rem, Shera, and Sylvie, they must actually think the horns were growing out of his head.

After all this time, it would be incredibly lame of him to tell them, "Actually, these come off," and remove them. The only time that would work is if it were some kind of beautiful, busty, crimson-eyed Demon Queen doing it.

To maintain his air of authority, he couldn't remove his horns.

Demons, as one of the races in this world, were born to Human parents, but somehow managed to receive the blood of the Fallen. As such, their bodies ended up covered in tattoo-like marks. Despite their physical abilities being lower in comparison to the other races, they excelled in using magic. And even though Demons were also one of the races descended from Celestials, they were especially subject to discrimination and persecution— At least, that was the setting for them in the game. In this world just the same, Diablo really had been on the receiving end of some pretty unfair treatment.

If Diablo had been a Human, he probably wouldn't be put under as much suspicion as he had until now.

Rem tugged at his sleeve. In a small voice, she whispered a warning to him.

"...You can't, Diablo... That is Faltra's insignia on his chest. It is proof he is one of the knights of this area. If things go sour, you could end up getting yourself arrested.

Shera huddled behind Diablo in fright.

"What? Is this guy someone scary?"

It wasn't like Diablo wanted to make this conversation become any worse than it already was. But that proved to be difficult when being told he was suspicious without having done anything.

"Hmph... It isn't like I set the town ablaze. What problem could he have with me?"

"What!? You're going to burn down the town!?"

"I haven't done anything yet."

"Hmmm!? 'Not yet,' you say!? So that means you're planning to do it!"

—*Dang. I really suck at talking with people.*

"Stop this nonsense… You're just going to say my horns make me seem suspicious, aren't you?"

The guard raised his voice.

"Not only that! Walking around in broad daylight with slaves in tow makes you even more questionable!"

"Slaves!?"

"Yes! Two beautiful young girls, at that! Despicable!"

—*What the hell!? Are you sure you're not just jealous!?*

On either side of Diablo, Shera and Rem hid their necks, embarrassed at being called slaves.

Unless it was times like these, it didn't seem to bother them as much anymore, but… Called "Enslavement Collars," these two unsightly bands wrapped around the girls' necks were usually meant for Summons after performing an "Enslavement Ritual." Due to Diablo's Demon Lord's Ring and its magic reflection ability, these collars ended up on the girls by accident when Diablo was summoned to this world.

The guard, who had no way of knowing this, mistook them for slaves instead.

—*I don't really get it, since there were no slaves back in the game. Is it weird to take them around in the middle of the day? Or is this guard just messed up in the head?*

If this was a colder region, then they could at least hide them with scarves or mufflers or something; but Faltra had a warm climate. It was temperate enough that you only needed one blanket to sleep at night.

Because of all this, of course the girls would be mistaken as slaves. But Diablo couldn't just keep quiet. He wanted to tell the guard that he wouldn't forgive anyone who called them slaves...

But how should he go about explaining this?

—*Telling him the whole story from the very beginning would be rough. I'm not good at talking for long periods of time anyways, so maybe I'll abbreviate it a bit.*

Hold on a sec... What exactly will I do if I don't forgive him? I should emphasize that part, just to get my point across better.

Thinking over his options, Diablo opened his mouth:

"I will destroy you so that not even one speck of ash remains."

—*Hm... Maybe I didn't say enough there?*

With a yell, the guard took a fighting stance with his halberd.

"Graaaah! So you show your true colors, you damn Fallen!"

Rem and Shera had started to panic.

"D-Diablo!? There is no need for you to get that upset! We are used to people misunderstanding why we have these!"

"That's right! Say what you like, but not even leaving ash behind makes me feel bad for him!"

"Stupid Shera, ash isn't the problem here!"

"W-Well, yeah! But if there's not even ash left, then it'd be really hard to make a grave for him, right!?"

Though the guard was wearing armor, anyone could tell he was starting to shake.

"Ngh... I'm going to be destroyed... by a Fallen... And they're talking about whether they should leave ash behind or not!? Damn it! Don't underestimate a knight of Faltra! Even if I can't run my blade through you, I can at least put up enough of a fight to let my comrades know of the proceeding danger!"

He was fully prepared for battle.

Diablo panicked.

—If things get any worse with this guy, I'm going to be investigated, aren't I?

If that happened, he would be taken away from Shera and he wouldn't be able to protect her.

Above all else, Diablo had to stop the Humans and Elves from going to war with each other. He didn't have time to be questioned by the guards.

—It's true the way I said that might have been bad… But I think that the guard is the strange one here for deciding I'm a Fallen. And all just because I have some horns and have two girls who look like slaves following me around.

This was a crucial time; they were on the brink of war.

—He should be able to forgive me. I'm the guy in charge of avoiding a war here, after all.

He shouldn't get so mad over me maybe going too far when I said that… Or not saying enough…

No way around it, I'll talk it out with him. I'm sure he'll understand then.

Steeling himself, Diablo decided to speak about the crisis this town was about to face:

"If you get in my way, I will turn this town into nothing but scorched earth."

"Damn you, Fallen! I won't forgive you!"

The guard raised his halberd overhead.

—*This is weird, right!? Why does everyone lose their temper like this!?*

He didn't feel like getting battered in a one-sided fight.

Reluctantly, Diablo took out Tenma's Staff. But just like with their assailants from earlier, it felt like he would kill this guy if he used magic.

—*What should I do?*

"Wait, wait, waaaaaait!! He may look it, but this person isn't dangerous!"

A small shadow wedged itself between Diablo and the guard; it was Sylvie.

The guard spoke out in surprise.

"Y-You're the Guildmaster, are you not!? Why are you covering for a Fallen!?"

"Just calm down, OK? He may have horns, but this person isn't a Fallen. He's on a quest from me and the governor, who we're here to meet with."

"...So he isn't a Fallen? And he isn't dangerous?"

"Y-Yeah... He's just your normal, everyday Demon... Probably. He's not dangerous, I think! Diablo, you're not dangerous, right? Boy, would I love to hear you say 'I'm not dangerous!'"

Sylvie glanced at him.

If she was going to say that much, then even Diablo couldn't mess this one up.

He gave placid nod.

"'I am not dangerous.'"

"Great! So that's that, then! We can go through, right? Riiiight?"

Clasping her hands together, Sylvie slightly tilted her head to the side as she asked.

The guard faltered.

"…S-So cute… Uh, I mean— U-Understood. If the Guildmaster herself says so, then I shall allow you to pass."

The guard lowered his halberd.

Sylvie, along with Rem and Shera, let out sighs of relief.

Diablo was relieved as well, but that attitude wouldn't be fitting of a Demon Lord. Instead, he bottled that feeling up inside himself and pressed onward.

"We're going!"

"Yeah, let's get going!"

"…Good grief."

"Hey, so… It'd be a problem if there was no ash left behind, right?"

Passing through the gate, Diablo and his three companions entered the Central District.

†

The governor's mansion—

In the very center of the Central District could be found a noticeably large mansion. It was built from bricks and was three stories high.

Ornate reliefs covered the windows and the doorways, and even the walls that surrounded the building had designs covering it. It was an impressive mansion.

Armored guards stood on either side of the front gate. As soon as Sylvie talked to them, Diablo and the others were shown through.

A steward from the mansion came up to them and respectfully bowed his head. Following him, they were led through a beautifully maintained garden; passed through the entrance; and were walked down a long hallway.

The floor here was covered in thick, red carpet. According to the game, this red color was only used in the residences of extremely important Humans, usually those of the highest levels of the upper-class aristocrats or royalty.

There hadn't been any event implemented in-game to meet the governor of Faltra, so this was the first time Diablo had come here. At the most, he had imagined this guy would be something like the mayor of this town, but it seemed like this person was of a much higher status.

The steward who had been guiding Diablo and the others knocked on the door.

"Master Galford, I have brought the Guildmaster and her companions."

For some reason, Diablo felt on edge, like he was on the verge of breaking into a boss room.

A grave yet composed voice answered from the other side of the door.

"Enter."

Just listening to the solemn voice made Diablo want to stand at attention.

The steward offered an apology for their intrusion, then opened the doors and stepped to the side.

It was a large room, covered in the same crimson carpet from the hall.

The wall directly in front of them contained a glass window; Diablo had never seen glass panes this large or undistorted since coming to this world.

The walls on either side of them were covered in bookshelves with elaborate designs. Books of various sizes lined these shelves, which reached all the way to the ceiling.

The bookshelf-lined walls also contained doors. If this were Cross Reverie, then these doors would be where the underlings of the boss would come out from to protect him.

—*Well, thinking about it normally, they would probably just lead to the bedroom and the study.*

In the center of the room was an extravagant table, with six chairs arranged around it. There was a large work desk here as well.

Standing with the flag of Faltra at his back and wearing a white military uniform, there was a Human male. Despite his middle-aged looks, he looked to be in the prime of his life.

The standard of culture for this world was based around the Middle Ages. Things like laundry detergent and bleach did not exist here. It was unthinkable for anyone but a truly exceptional person to wear a high-class commodity such as white clothing; especially so as a military uniform, something that could easily get dirtied.

He wore his black hair short, as you would expect of military personnel; and wrinkles creased the corners of his eyes and forehead.

The glint in his eyes would be enough to make a monster run away in fear.

"Hm… So, is it finished?"

—*Is what finished, exactly?* Diablo didn't understand what he meant.

Sylvie gave a bitter laugh.

"For now, I had Diablo here take on that quest for us."

The governor narrowed his eyes.

"So, he's taken on the task. Then you should solve this matter quickly. You can report to me after the job is finished."

—*So that "Is it finished?" from earlier was actually supposed to mean, "Did you stop the war?"*

If this were the game, he could pass this off as, "Oh, this NPC just talks this way;" but the people living in this world were alive, and could think for themselves.

—*Just how hasty is this guy?*

Diablo just couldn't bring himself to understand how this man would even think to ask such a thing of them. For such a ridiculously difficult task to be completed when not even half a day had gone by.

Sylvie tried to put everyone at ease.

"Um, you see… This is a pretty difficult quest, you know? I thought we could get some information."

"I believe I already explained everything you needed to know."

"Well, about that…"

"As I thought, Adventurers cannot be relied on after all. Though they act proud and swagger around town, they make excuses and run away when faced with real danger. In the end, it seems that the army are the ones who will protect this country."

—*What was that?*

Diablo gripped his staff.

Sylvie stepped in front of him, waving her hands.

"Oh no! Not at all! I won't run away, and Diablo is looking forward to tackling this quest!"

"If that's the case, then hurry up and drive these Elves away."

"Yes, of course! I don't think it should take too long… Probably. Um… Oh, that's right! Do you think that perhaps you could give them a little self-introduction?"

Sylvie seemed to be taking great care when she spoke. Not to mention the governor was overbearing.

Diablo didn't know exactly how great and important this guy was, but surely Sylvie shouldn't have to act this way towards him. It was clear he looked down on Adventurers.

It was pissing Diablo off.

But because of the governor's overbearing presence, he would end up averting his eyes if he didn't keep himself focused.

—*I can't let him see me acting weak here.*

If the governor decided that Diablo was not meant to be feared, then he might attack on the spot. Diablo had to make him think that a confrontation between them would be a bad thing.

Diablo glared at the governor.

The governor began to speak: "What trouble… So an Adventurer doesn't know the name of the governor."

"He only just arrived in Faltra the other day."

"Then remember this well… I am Lieutenant General Chester Ray Galford. I am in charge of the Stronghold City of Faltra, under orders from His Majesty the King."

"Hmph… So you're the governor who just stood idly by and watched while Fallen attacked his town."

When the Fallen Gregore had appeared in town the other day, Diablo had been the one to come rushing in to destroy him, not the governor nor his army.

One could almost hear as Galford ground his back teeth together.

"…Before I could receive a report, the situation had calmed down. That is all. I do not find there to be a problem with that."

"Lucky for you, wasn't it?"

Hiding the fact he was practically shivering on the inside, the corners of Diablo's mouth twisted into a smile.

He couldn't recall anyone named "Galford." They might have been mentioned in the lore of Cross Reverie, but Diablo didn't remember the names of NPCs who didn't have events associated with them.

Attempting to lower the tension in the room, Rem politely introduced herself.

"My name is Rem Galleu. I am a level 40 Adventurer, and a Summoner. U-Um, this person does not mean any ill-will, and—"

Galford raised a hand to interrupt her.

"I am already fully aware that Adventurers lack manners."

"…Forgive me."

"Young Rem Galleu, you should consider your place of work. I have heard the Mage's Association has extended you an invitation to join them. You mustn't be planning on being an Adventurer forever."

"…Th-That may be true, but I have my own reasons for continuing on as I have."

It was quite an extreme way to put things on the governor's part. Not only were there other Adventurers in the room, but the Guildmaster herself was here.

Sylvie smiled bitingly.

"That's pretty harsh of you."

"One of my subordinates has been carrying out an investigation on you all. It seems you've been causing some problems around here."

"…Problems?"

"Threatening a guard on the Bridge of Ulug, destroying the stone roads and buildings with magic in the southern avenues... I wouldn't expect this kind of irreproachable conduct from Adventurers."

"There was a reason for all that!"

Shera raised an objection along with Rem.

"That's right! Diablo isn't at fault here!"

"But the fact remains, then, that you do not deny it happening."

With a small whimper, Rem and Shera went silent.

Galford was a man that acted like a strict teacher. He didn't have an ounce of faith in Adventurers, and seemed to especially hate Diablo.

They were engulfed in this man's presence. Diablo wanted to avoid staying here for any long period of time. Now was be the time to quickly switch to the main topic at hand.

—But before that, I have to introduce myself. It seems like he already knows my name, but he did just tell me his. Etiquette demands that this be the bare minimum of courtesy I can offer him.

To maintain his air of authority, he couldn't stop his Demon Lord act. Diablo wanted to avoid making the governor any angrier than he already was. Diablo wouldn't be able to get any information from him if that happened, and since this person didn't seem to particularly like Diablo, he had to be even more careful than usual.

—Let's do this normally.

He was aiming to be normal here.

Normal.

"I am Diablo. I came to speak with you."

—How was that!? That was nice and amicable, wasn't it! I really can do it if I try!

He made a quick peek to see Rem and Shera's reactions, but they didn't seem particularly surprised.

Diablo was striking victory poses on the inside at the fact he had managed to do a harmless self-introduction.

Galford's gaze was focused on Diablo, as if he were evaluating Diablo's worth.

"First, there is one thing I wish to ask. You proclaim yourself a Demon Lord from another world, or something of the like… Is that true?"

It was a loaded question, as if Galford was provoking him. The Demon Lord role play ingrained deep into his body exploded out of him all at once.

"Heh heh heh… Shall I turn you into burnt charcoal as proof?"

Diablo glared back at him.

—*AAaaaAAaaAHHHHhhHHHhhHH!!*

That was all his fault! He was the who set the mood, that's why I got so into it!

In a panic, Rem and Shera jumped at him, latching onto his arms.

"W-Wait, Diablo!"

"That's right! Ash is bad, but charcoal is bad, too!"

"Oh dear…"

Sylvie's face had gone completely pale. It looked like she could fall over at any moment.

Galford slowly and deliberately closed the gap between them.

—*Is he planning on fighting me like this!? Can I win in a one-on-one fight?*

Things will get bad fast if he calls more soldiers... Should I just run away?

A cold sweat broke out on Diablo's back; but even so, he kept an arrogant smile on his face.

The governor stepped directly in front of him.

"As long as you complete the mission I assign you, I do not care if you are a Demon Lord or whatnot. Are you an asset to the land I govern? Or are you a liability? That is the only thing that matters."

"Hmph... I'm only helping you because I feel like it. Do not mistake yourself into thinking you can control me."

"Hm... Just as I thought, you Adventurers are quite the collection of misfits."

It felt like he wasn't just mocking Diablo, but all Adventurers when he said that.

In short, this guy had decided that Diablo was a freak, and that him being a "Demon Lord from another world" was all something he had made up in his head.

—Well, I guess he'd be right on that point... But would he believe me any more if I told him that I was a player summoned in my character's likeness from Cross Reverie?

His desire to hole himself up somewhere started to bubble to the surface.

—I just want to lock myself in my room and play games all day. Then I wouldn't have to deal with adults who have sticks up their asses like this guy...

No, I have to tough this one out.

If Diablo was going to protect Shera, then it would be best not to antagonize Galford. The governor acted in this manner most likely because he himself knew he was not someone to be trifled with.

"Governor, spare me this nonsense... If you desire to see your wish fulfilled, then tell me what you know."

Diablo did not drop his high-and-mighty attitude.

The same went for the governor, who coolly nodded.

"You have already heard the demands of the Kingdom of Greenwood, I imagine? The request to turn over Princess Shera came in two days ago."

"Two days ago... The deadline was set for ten days later, correct?"

"There are only eight days left."

Are you freakin' kidding me? Diablo retorted on the inside. *If he didn't make that part clear, it could have led to me failing miserably. Does he even want to avoid a war?*

Galford calmly continued his explanation.

"There have also been reports of Elf sightings near the 《Eastern Lakefront》. Do you understand the layout of that area?"

"Of course. I could even lead you into the deepest parts of the Demon Lord's territory."

"Oh hoh?"

"Only if you do not value your life, that is."

He had all the maps for Cross Reverie in his head— Though the features from the maps in-game might not all be the same as in this world.

The 《Eastern Lakefront》 was located southeast of the town. To the west of Faltra, there was something called 《Seplia Lake》. You could find it by walking just past the farmlands located outside the city walls. The forest to the east of Seplia Lake was the Eastern Lakefront.

Galford turned his gaze to the map on the desk.

"I do not know how many Elves are located there. Their specialty is concealing themselves within the forest, you see."

Elves had a particularly high Sneak skill, and when in the forest, they were better at concealing themselves than Grasswalkers. They could sneak up unnoticed, and fire volleys of arrows from tree shadows or from the top of tree branches.

In the game, Sneak would allow the user to not show up on the radar (a feature that showed the locations of other players or monsters). There was nothing as convenient as a radar in this world, so the only thing one could rely on were vague abilities like sensing presences. An opponent with a high Sneak skill in this world was much more dangerous than if it happened in the game.

"Have you not even scouted them out?"

"Even if I sent a small team to perform reconnaissance, this is an enemy skilled at surprise attacks. That would only lead to more casualties. The witness who found the Elves was a townsperson who had been hunting in the forest, and luckily managed to get back safely. According to their report, there were about twenty Elves... But I'm sure their numbers are greater. If they were a squad of one hundred or more, however, then we would most certainly know, even if they were hiding. Even considering Greenwood's power and influence, I am positive they wouldn't assemble a force that large. At most, I'd say there are a hundred of them. That is all the information I have received."

"One hundred of them... That's not a lot for an army... But very convenient for me. They should pose no threat."

"Hmph," the governor snorted.

"Though Greenwood may call themselves a 'Kingdom,' in the end they are only a small faction."

"So you don't think of them as a threat?"

Galford shook his head after a slight pause.

"No... I would never underestimate my enemy. If I sent my own forces into the forest, where the Elves are lying in wait, I would lose countless soldiers. What I abhor the most is sending my own subordinates to a meaningless death."

His voice sounded dispassionate, so it was hard to tell what he was feeling. But Diablo felt that the governor had spoken those last words with extra force.

—*Obviously a commander wouldn't want to lose so many of his subordinates.*

"So that's why you wish to use me."

"It wouldn't be necessary if you handed over the princess."

"I refuse!"

"...Is Princess Shera so important to you?"

Shera turned to look at Diablo at the governor's question. Though the two had talked plenty about the subject, it seemed she was still worried.

"Hmph... Don't ask such foolish things. It's one thing if she herself says she will leave... But I have no intention of turning a blind eye to her being stolen away by someone else."

"There is certainly no reason to yield to the likes of Elves. Personally, I have no intention of just willingly giving into the Kingdom of Greenwood's demands. Words should be met with words... and force should be met with force."

"That's only natural."

With a nod, Galford turned to look at Shera, pausing his conversation with Diablo.

"That's right... There was something I wanted to ask you if I had the chance to meet you."

"Something to ask me?" Shera tilted her head.

"What did you want so badly that would make you throw away your life of luxury, going so far to take on the dangerous life of an Adventurer? Or, perhaps, did you have a reason you couldn't stay in your homeland?"

Silence.

Shera had a pensive look on her face.

"...I wanted freedom. I didn't really know how to obtain it, but... I wanted a reason for existing. I wanted to know my own worth, and not as a part of my lineage or as part of the Elven royal family. I felt that I wouldn't be able to obtain that back home."

"I see... From a poor man's perspective, it may seem like you lived a life of luxury; but it's true that all people, regardless of their upbringing, have different circumstances and senses of value."

"Do you understand now?"

"I cannot sympathize with you. I will, however, remember it as valuable information."

"I see..."

Shera's shoulders slumped.

Certainly, it had to be difficult to lead a life in this world where one did not have to worry about food or their life being in danger. It must have been hard to agree with Shera's actions when she had thrown that all away for the sake of freedom.

But Diablo was different. In his world, he didn't have to worry about what he would eat for the day, let alone being attacked by monsters. That's why he could understand Shera's feelings— Or at least, he felt he could.

Grabbing Shera's shoulders, Diablo pulled her close to himself.

"There is no need for you to seek sympathy from others... I shall allow as such. Put yourself through as many hardships as you like, exert yourself as hard as you like, and push yourself to the limit as much as you like. Savor the fruits of labor that you earned with your own two hands— That is what it means to live a life of freedom."

"Y-Yeah!"

A smile broke out on Shera's face.

Rem nodded, while Sylvie smiled warmly.

It was a declaration—one in which he proclaimed that he would protect her.

—*That's all fine and dandy, but how am I going to deal with the Elven troops?*

Before, when they had attempted to take Shera away, it was the elite Elf Celsior who had come for her. He had hidden himself in the forest along with about ten of his subordinates, but Shera was the one who sensed he and his comrades were waiting for them. Diablo and Rem hadn't noticed anything in the slightest.

Could Diablo properly fight against them?

He hadn't acquired anything he could use to negotiate with the Elves.

—*So that means things are like this:*

"Give us back the princess!" say the Elves.

"I refuse!" says Diablo.

"Like hell I would listen to what the Elves say," says the governor. "But my soldiers are important to me, so I leave this to you."

There was only one outcome that could come of this:

"Then this means war!" cry the Elves.

—*What a pain in the ass...* It was enough to make his head hurt. Rem sighed.

"…Avoiding a war… If only we had some kind of 'treasure' of equal value to Shera that would satisfy the Kingdom of Greenwood… Then we would at least be able to try and negotiate with them…"

Shera proudly stuck out her chest.

"Mh-hm-hm! I wasn't called the 'most valuable asset of the Elves' for nothing, after all! I don't think there's anything that could replace me!"

"…On second thought, we should just return this dumb Elf. For the sake of peace."

"What!? Why are you mad all of a sudden!"

Rem sighed again.

"Then, we will not turn over Princess Shera. You will all take measures to avoid a war with the Kingdom of Greenwood, and the reward shall be paid through the Adventurer's Guild— Are we in agreement?" Galford asked in confirmation.

"Hmph… Shera was in my possession from the beginning. I will not allow others to interfere."

"Then I leave this to you."

Turning his gaze to the door on his right, Galford continued to speak.

"That is all I have to say to you as governor of Faltra… But in regard to this situation, the Royal Capital has also dispatched one of their own. Allow me to introduce them."

†

The door opened, and a tall woman entered the room.

She had a slim body, and long, slender arms and legs. Her red hair reached down to her waist, and the thin green glasses she wore gave her an intellectual impression.

The armor she wore was light and seemed easy to move in. Some sort of cloak covered it, but the top of her armor left her shoulders exposed. Diablo had seen the design of her armor somewhere before.

At a glance, it looked like she had an icy-cold stare… But when she smiled, she gave off such a friendly atmosphere that it put Diablo at ease. It made him feel like smiling himself.

The girl gave a salute by placing her left hand on her chest.

"A pleasure to make your acquaintance. My name is Alicia Cristela, an Imperial Knight. His Majesty the King has bestowed upon me the task of resolving the situation with the Kingdom of Greenwood. Please forgive some of my inexperience, but I will do my absolute best to be of use to you all. I look forward to working with you."

She was extremely polite.

—*So, she's an Imperial Knight.*

These soldiers had made appearances in the game as NPCs. According to the game's setting, they were knights who came from families of high pedigrees and showed considerable skill. Above all, they were under the direct control of the King himself.

They had roles and authority in-game similar to police. They would move from town to town, or stay on the outskirts, with their purpose being to protect citizens from criminals or monsters. But unlike the army, they would not invade enemy territory. Compared to them, the Imperial Knights were more like "military police" than soldiers.

In the world of Cross Reverie, they were treated as "noble knights admired and respected by the people."

"…A female Imperial Knight is extremely rare to see," Rem said in surprise.

Shera seemed to be of the same opinion as well.

"I know, right? I always thought of the Imperial Knights as being all Human guys."

—*All Human guys, huh.*

The setting of the game had stated there were many problems in the world concerning gender discrimination. Though they were just trying to make it seem more like the outlook of a world from the Middle Ages, people thought the creators of Cross Reverie might have been promoting sexism themselves. That's why, regardless of whether you chose to play as a male or female character in Cross Reverie, there were no differences in abilities or equipment between genders. There was nothing about the game that emphasized the discrimination against women outlined in the game's setting.

Sometimes during quests, however, you would see phrases like, "Female Imperial Knights are rare" and "It's hard for women to get appointed as one." Based on what Rem and Shera had said—

It was most likely men who held positions of power in this world. Positions of honor and responsibility were also most likely assigned to men, with women receiving unfair treatment in this regard.

Because the Guildmaster Sylvie was both a Demi and a woman, there wasn't much discrimination coming from Adventurers. Diablo didn't feel any discrimination from the townspeople in everyday life, either.

—*I guess that would make it a value held by those in power here.*

But, there were a whole bunch of "rare female Imperial Knights" who appeared in quests in-game, though.

Whenever an Imperial Knight showed up, most of the time it was to give the player, an Adventurer, a quest. If a male Imperial Knight told you to work on his behalf just to make him look better, then of course you wouldn't want to do it.

A majority of the players were guys, though most of the characters were girls. (That's part of the dark side of MMORPGs, so enough about that for now.)

Taking a quest from a cute girl was much better motivation than from a self-important old dude. Many more players would even pay cold hard cash just so they could finish these quests within the time limit.

On that subject, there were ultra-hard quests offered by an NPC who was called the "Devilish Imperial Knight, Miss Miyuri." She had big boobs, a bobbed haircut, and was so timid that it seemed like she would cry at any time when asking for your help. If you were moved by her plea and took on the quest, there would usually be a gigantic monster or something waiting for you when you went to the specified dungeon.

Many a beginner had become monster food thanks to her quests.

—*I wonder if she's in this world, too?*

Alicia spoke in a gentle tone of voice.

"It is quite unusual, isn't it. I am fortunate enough to be both a woman and to serve as an Imperial Knight."

"...That is a wonderful thing. I am certain you worked very hard to get where you are now."

Rem may have felt that way because she too had hardships she could not share with others.

"Thank you very much. It's true that I face some difficulties because I am a woman... but I still have a long way to go. It seems that you have your own problems you are struggling with, too, Miss Rem."

"…Why do you think that?"

On guard, Rem cautiously took a step back.

Alicia waved both her hands in front of herself.

"I'm sorry, just a guess on my part. According to the reports, you are a very capable Summoner in possession of seven Summons. But despite that, you will not enter the Mage's Association; and you will not work for the governor, either. That's why I thought you must have a reason for that."

"…Indeed, that is quite a logical way of thinking."

"I have no intention of prying into you, Miss Rem. My goal is to iron out the problem the city of Faltra is facing."

"…All right."

"But you are also a citizen of Faltra, Miss Rem. If I can be of any help to you whatsoever, please feel free to consult with me. Though I may have an obligation as an Imperial Knight, I especially worry about people such as you who keep their struggles to themselves. You do not need to force yourself to tell me your secret, however."

"…I see… For now, I will just accept those sentiments."

It looked as if she had rejected Alicia, but she did not deny that she was harboring a secret. Rem must have had a somewhat decent amount of trust in Alicia.

Alicia shifted her gaze to Shera.

"Miss Shera, I am sure you must be going through a lot because of this, but let's do our best to make everyone happy!"

"Yeah! Let's do our best together!"

Shera smiled ear-to-ear.

Alicia then turned to Sylvie: "This is an expression of sympathy from His Majesty." She handed over a leather pouch filled with gold coins. This was probably reparation for all the Adventurers who had lost their lives to the Fallen, Gregore.

Diablo was working hard to not let his admiration show on his face.

—*She's so damn good at talking with people!*

It wasn't that she was just nice: though she didn't know what Rem's circumstances were, she still theoretically made an offer to help her; for Shera, she had chosen to use words that were simple and easy to understand; in recognition of Sylvie's position as Guildmaster, she had brought something to offer to her.

While she may have heard some of their conversation from inside the other room, and even though it was her first time meeting them all, she was able to quickly adjust how she interacted with everyone.

Alicia fixed her eyes on Diablo.

She was quite the beauty. It seemed like he could get sucked into her eyes at any time.

Diablo felt a kind of nervousness different than when he had confronted Galford. He tried to pass it off by snorting.

"Hmph… Do you have something you want to say?"

"Please, let me express my gratitude to you."

"Express gratitude… to me?"

"You exterminated Gregore, the Fallen who appeared in Faltra, and saved the head of the Mage's Association, Celestine Baudelaire. Not only that, but you also repelled the one hundred Fallen who advanced on the Bridge of Ulug… As an Imperial Knight charged with protecting and keeping the citizens of this country safe, I cannot help but feel appreciation and respect towards you. Thank you very much."

Being thanked so sincerely was making him uncomfortable.

"Ah… That was… I destroyed those Fallen because they had dared to oppose me. I do not care about the lives of the other races."

—Oops, maybe that part about not caring about the lives of others was saying too much.

Diablo would often regret something he just said. He wasn't very good at talking.

But it seemed Alicia did not mind.

"I see. I do not think that you would need assistance or anything of the sort, but I have a duty to report to His Majesty until this matter is resolved. So please, allow me to stay by your side until then."

"…Do as you wish."

There was nothing else he could say back.

The Imperial Knights were elites. Their family background and abilities were leagues above the average members of the other races. In spite of all that, she was treating Diablo, a Demon who was also an Adventurer, with the utmost respect and courtesy…

—So this is what it looks like to be a natural at talking with others…

Truly frightening.

If he let his guard down, then she might see through his Demon Lord role play as just an act.

This might be his most fearsome enemy yet.

—I'll make sure to threaten her so she doesn't try to talk to me too often, thought Diablo.

He deliberately made his voice deep:

"If you do not wish to die, then do not speak to me so carelessly."

Alicia's eyes widened in shock. He thought that would be enough to scare her, but instead, she gave a deep nod.

"Then I shall prepare myself for that... You have protected the citizens of Lyferia from a grave danger that threatened the entire country. My life is a small price to pay if it will quell your anger."

"Uh..."

Diablo was at a loss for words.

Rem and Shera stared at each other, similarly dumbfounded.

Sylvie shrugged her shoulders, while Galford cleared his throat.

"It would be a problem for me if you just went and died so easily... His Majesty would boil me alive for that. Alicia Cristela is the daughter of a duke, a talented woman who graduated top of her class at the Knight Academy—and a favorite of the King. Normally, I would never allow her to work alongside the likes of Adventurers... But, unfortunately, I do not have the authority to issue orders to Imperial Knights."

Alicia bowed her head: "I apologize for any trouble I will cause you."

—So basically, she's no ordinary Imperial Knight.

Galford rang a small bell on top of his desk.

"Now if you will excuse me, I have a meeting to attend."

The door to the room opened, and the steward who had first guided Diablo and the others came in, once again respectfully lowering his head.

—And now he's telling us to get lost.

But this was already enough for Diablo.

He had learned of the Elves' location and the size of their troops, as well as the deadline for the quest. He also discovered how the governor thought as well. This was almost a perfect score in terms of information gathering—

As long as you didn't include the fact that he had no specific plan to deal with this situation, that is.

†

Taking their leave from the governor's estate, Diablo and the others walked through the Central District.

After exiting through the southern gate, Sylvie stepped away from the group.

"I'm gonna head back to the Adventurer's Guild, then. If you ever need a place to sleep, feel free to come over anytime, OK?"

"Um, thank you for everything!" Shera spoke up. "I'm going to try my best to do everything I can to make sure the war doesn't happen!"

"I didn't do anything you need to thank me for. All I did was fulfill the Adventurer's Guild's role of bringing together the client and the Adventurer who's doing their request. I'm not a fan of wars myself, so I'm counting on you, Diablo."

"Yeah! If it's Diablo doing it, I'm sure it'll be all right! Oh, but I'll be trying super hard to do my best too, of course!" Shera cheered, clenching her fists together.

—*The Diablo you're talking about is having one hell of a time trying to figure out what he should be doing though, you know…*

They were counting on him. But he was a Sorcerer, not a tactician. He couldn't just think up a way to avoid a war.

As if she had remembered something, Sylvie came closer to Diablo and beckoned to him.

—*Looks like she wants me to bend down.* The difference between their heights was fairly large, so if they were both standing, like they were, they couldn't keep their conversation private.

As soon as he bent over, Sylvie brought her lips close to his ears.

"So, I think you already know this… But there's been people watching us for a while now, right?"

—Where!?

He couldn't sense anything around them; they had passed through the Central District and other relatively unpopulated areas, but he hadn't noticed at all.

—I need that radar in the top-right corner of my screen, dang it!

But if he were to be honest and say "I had no idea," that would not only be lame, but not very Demon Lord-esque, either.

"…So it seems. What a foolish thing for them to do."

He muttered these words as if they were the most trifling things in the world.

"Those are observers sent by the governor himself, but don't hurt them or anything, OK? It's not like you have to protect them, but don't drive them away, either."

Of course he wouldn't do that… Though a Demon Lord *would* say something like "What an eyesore" and attack them.

"Hmph… It's not even worth dealing my judgment upon them."

"Then that's a good thing! That's it for me, then. See ya around!"

Waving goodbye, Sylvie headed back towards the Adventurer's Guild.

Seeing her run into the distance was like watching a kid going back home from the playground—though her outfit exposed just a liiiittle too much for that image. That would definitely be a cause for concern.

Sylvie moved so fast that she disappeared from their sight almost immediately.

"…Sylvie is a good person. I have never even spoken with her that much before," Rem said quietly.

"It seems that way."

"…I do not dislike Faltra. Because it is on the front lines, people support each other, it's lively, and the entire town feels alive. All the townspeople here would not want a war between races."

Shera cheerfully agreed with her, while Alicia gave a nod.

—*And I feel the same way.*

But a peace-loving Demon Lord would be kind of weird, so he kept his mouth shut.

—*Wait a second… So now Sylvie's left our party. This is bad.*

Now they no longer had a way to deal with future attackers. Her Bind magic was truly powerful, and Diablo wasn't sure yet if he could rely on Alicia as a replacement for it.

On the contrary, if Diablo ended up killing someone, there would be an Imperial Knight right by him… It was possible he'd be arrested on the spot.

He couldn't rely on the governor's warm-hearted kindness if that happened.

—*How can I fend off attackers now?*

It would be the same problem if he ended up fighting with the Elves.

Rem and the others all hated the idea of war. That wasn't just because they were citizens of Faltra, but also because they didn't want to kill other people. After all, the Elves were from Shera's hometown.

Unlike when he was facing off against the army of one hundred Fallen, he couldn't hit them with a White Nova, annihilating them so that not even ash remained.

—*What about a weapon?*

Diablo may be a Sorcerer, but he had also hit the level cap of 150. His STR and AGI stats were higher than any lower level Warriors. His magic was too strong, which made it hard to use, but a weapon might be effective in holding himself back. It would also be convenient for taking on a great deal of people at once. He would be able to fight without using MP.

When he lost MP, his energy would start to wither. If he used it all, then he wouldn't be able to keep going on. He would end up idling around all day; and before he knew it, he would be hungry, and the sun would be setting.

First, he had to protect himself before he could think about avoiding a war.

He decided to head to the weapons shop.

"Come with me."

He flipped his cape around and started to walk.

In a slight haste, Rem trotted up beside him.

"…Where are you going? As your Summoner, I would like an explanation before you do something."

Shera, who had been warily listening to the conversation, raised her voice.

"Excuse me!? No talking about Diablo like he's your Summon! I'm the one who summoned him! Me! It was me!!"

Now this was nostalgic.

—*They're still doing this?*

Alicia had a curious look on her face.

"Um… Was Sir Diablo really summoned by either Miss Rem or Miss Shera?"

"…I am his Summoner."

"And I said I am! I was the one who said we should summon a Demon Lord from another world, after all!"

"Miss Shera, why did you consider summoning a Demon Lord in the first place?"

"I mean, a Demon Lord has got to be the strongest there is, right? And I needed a strong Summon."

"Were you not afraid?"

"Huh? Summons have to listen to what their Summoners say, so it's all good, right?"

"But…"

In reality, Shera and Rem had been stuck with enslavement collars, while Diablo, the self-proclaimed Demon Lord, strutted about town with the girls.

Alicia started to bombard Shera with questions, things like, "Where did you summon him?" and "Under what conditions?" Diablo wondered if she was going to report all this to the King as well. Being an Imperial Knight seemed like it was a surprisingly straightforward, yet busy line of work.

Rem tried asking again.

"…And where exactly is our destination?"

"We're not going to the forest where all the Elves are, are we!?"

Avoiding Alicia's questions, Shera asked one of her own.

Diablo smiled.

"Before that, we must go to the weapons shop."

"The weapons shop…?" the girls asked in unison.

"…But why? I do not believe you will find anything better than the remarkable staff you own lying around in one of the shops here."

"Yeah! And the shops in town only have swords and spears and stuff. Nothing here is enchanted, either."

"Don't come to conclusions based on your own inferior standards. I have an idea."

"If I'm going to be up against more attackers or Elves, I need to buy a weapon that makes it easy for me to hold myself back." —Is something considerate that a Demon Lord would never say.

He really wanted to go by himself, but right now, it was impossible for him to leave Shera alone.

Having Rem guide him, Diablo headed towards the southern shopping district.

"Well, whatever, I guess!" Shera said happily as she followed along.

Without questions or complaints, Alicia accompanied close behind them.

†

The weapons shop—

There were plenty of shops lined up along the street in Faltra's Southern District. This was where you could find most of the things you would need as an Adventurer.

The weapons shop was a stone building, and though it was a shop, the front of the building wasn't left wide open or anything. They opened the heavy door, which was larger than the average house's, and entered the store.

The inside was spacious, and smelled of iron.

One thing that stood out about the interior was that they had used bricks, a high-quality building material here.

—*Looks like they might be doing pretty well for themselves.*

There was an employee behind the counter, and an array of weapons behind them.

—*I guess I have to ask the employee over there to show me each weapon one at a time.*

That was an obvious precaution for them to take. Public order here was a lot worse compared to 21st century Japan.

It hadn't even been half a month since he came here, but he had already gotten used to how unnatural it felt to see things like swords and bladed weapons hung up in display cases.

The employee here was a female Grasswalker. She had a bandana tied around her head, with two long rabbit ears poking out from between the gaps in the fabric. Since she was part of a race that looked childlike even after reaching adulthood, her age was a mystery.

She wore a durable hemp shirt as part of her work clothes. Diablo couldn't see the bottom-half of her, but her outfit screamed "blacksmith."

—*That was the NPC from the weapons shop in-game, right?*

If anything, she looked a whole lot like the NPC, at least.

—*If I remember right, according to the game's setting, she was supposed to be a blacksmith's apprentice.*

She was said to have entered into an apprenticeship under the Dwarf who ran the shop, whom she looked up to and admired. She didn't actually get to take up the hammer much, however, and was always forced to work at the front counter instead. Sometimes she would try to forge things in secret, but her master would yell at her once he found out.

She had two ways of greeting customers: the "normal" version, and the "after she was yelled at" version.

Diablo called out to the girl behind the counter:

"I came to look at your weapons."

"Waaaaaahhh! We've got lots of great weapons heeeeere! I haven't gotten to make a single one though, goddammittttttt!"

It was the "after she was yelled at" version.

—*This part is just like the game... Strange.*

But there must have been plenty of other weapon shops around here. There weren't any NPCs named Rem, Shera, or Sylvie, for that matter, and the Guildmaster never even made an appearance in-game. It felt like Diablo was progressing through a quest yet unknown to him in the world of Cross Reverie. It wasn't clear yet just how much this world differed from the game.

Diablo didn't know what to do to calm down the Grasswalker employee, so he decided to just ignore it and tell her the features of the weapon he wanted.

"Listen, and listen well— I am searching for a weapon that does not look out of place to carry around town, that needs no maintenance whatsoever, and has a sufficiently attractive appearance to behold."

"Do you mean a longsword, hmmmm!? We've got some good ones here! I didn't make any of them thoooooough!"

"Hm… A longsword, as I thought."

The first thing a player would do after picking a Warrior class in Cross Reverie was buy a sword. Races with lower STR stats would buy daggers, though.

There weren't any weird tricks to using it, and was a breeze to handle. Being able to buy a relatively powerful weapon for cheap was one of its charms.

By the way, there were no equipment restrictions in Cross Reverie. A Sorcerer could use a longsword, and could even equip metal armor. However, while most staffs worked to buff your magic in some way, there were no swords that offered those kinds of perks. The same went for armor, as they were not suitable equipment for Sorcerers.

If you were to choose equipment based on stats, a Sorcerer would end up with a robe and staff. But since you wouldn't know unless you gave it a shot yourself, Diablo had tested out using swords and spears and the like, so he wasn't a complete amateur with them— in the game, at least. He had already experienced how strong his STR stat was here, but he wouldn't be able to tell how well he could use a sword in this world unless he tried.

Rem nodded as if she had just figured something out.

"…I see now. It's a weapon to drive back attackers without killing them."

"Wha-huh? What do you mean?"

"…Do you not understand, Shera? If Diablo uses his magic against Adventurers like them, their lives are as good as forfeit. If he uses a weapon, then Diablo would be able to stop right on the verge of killing them."

"Oho! I see!"

"…It seems Diablo is kind after all."

"Yeah, he is!"

Rem and Shera stared at him like they were looking at a kitten or something.

He wanted to deny what they had said, but couldn't come up with a snappy retort. He made a displeased "Hmph" as he snorted through his nose.

Diablo spoke to the employee.

"I will take a sword. Show me what you—"

He stopped in the middle of his sentence. A certain something had caught his eye.

It was a weapon leaning against the wall in the back. It had a length that spanned over two meters, and sported a long handle, like one you would find on a spear. From end to end, it was made of pure black iron with one long, curved blade attached to it. It had an ominous, warped blade, as if the iron had been made in the shape of a demon's wing.

A "Great Scythe."

It was a huge scythe, like the ones a Grim Reaper from a game or anime would have. Diablo couldn't take his eyes off it.

—That is too cool!!

It was perfect for a Demon Lord. He was taken with it in an instant.

Usually, he would look at its stats and reject it for being too weak… But this time, being weak was a good thing. In fact, it would be a problem if it wasn't weak.

Just by looking at it, one could tell it was a weapon for those who cared about appearances—and *only* appearances.

Diablo pointed to the scythe against the wall.

"Show me that one."

"…And which one would that beeeee… Huh? By that one, do you mean… that war scythe?"

"Correct."

"…I'm the one who forged that one, but… The balance is all off, there's no sharpness to the blade, and its design is so distasteful that my master scolded me for it, saying 'This ain't no toy store!' A real gem, I know, but what about it? If you're going to laugh at me for it, could you go do it somewhere else?"

"Give me that."

"Excuse me, sir, but are you insane!?"

"Do you not understand? It is perfect for me."

"But sir, you said you were looking for a weapon that 'does not look out of place to carry around town, that needs no maintenance whatsoever, and has a sufficiently attractive appearance to behold,' right?"

"Yes."

"But if you walked around town with that, it would definitely look weird, and you have to keep sharpening the blade when you use it, and only people with awful taste would like that design… I'm tearing up just saying that. Is this some kind of next level bullying or something?"

"Hmph… Your way of thinking is too shallow."

"Huh?"

"Think about it. Would that weapon look strange if I was the one holding it?"

The employee went silent.

And then—

"It would look totally natural!?"

"But of course. I was planning on using it so as not to strike with the blade, so maintenance will not be necessary. And if I'm the one holding it, then it should not appear strange."

"If you're planning on not using the blade, then why a scythe!? —Is what I want to say, but you're right. It perfectly matches with how you look… But why are you dressed up like a Fallen, anyways?"

"Do not pry any further. That war scythe perfectly suits me, and you shall sell it to me. Any problems with that?"

"It's true that there's no one else that creepy scythe would look better on than you… A-All right, understood! I'm a blacksmith too, after all! A blacksmith-in-training, though! If you say that you want something I made that much, then I can't just *not* give it to you, riiiiight! To be honest, I was wondering how I was going to get rid of the thing, so you can give me how much it cost for the steel to make it: one silver coin!"

—*That's way too cheap.*

He was planning on heading to the item shop after this, however, so it helped if he could keep his expenses low here. He had received a sizable reward for completing Celes's errand quest the other day, but because all he had been doing was laze around and sleep since then, he was uneasy about his funds.

There was also talk of a reward for saving the town from the Fallen, Gregore— But since he was in full-on apathy mode after using too much of his MP, he had turned it down because he thought it was too much of a pain to deal with.

Taking a leather bag out of his pouch, he handed over a silver coin as payment.

For reference, one silver coin turned out to be 4,000 friths. That was about the same for a night at the Peace of Mind Inn, dinner included. You needed 200,000 friths for the average longsword, at the very least.

The girl clutched the silver coin, as if she were treasuring it.

"Th-This is the first time… I've sold a weapon I made… Thank you so much, sir! I'll go grab it for you, so just wait a sec, OK?"

Looking like she was having some trouble carrying it, she huffed and puffed as she brought it over to Diablo.

He took it from her.

—*This thing's pretty heavy.*

Diablo's STR stat should have been fairly high, but even so, it weighed heavy on him. The blade was too thick, and the handle was too long.

Looking closer at it, the edge was wave-bladed, like a flamberge. The wounds after taking a hit from this would definitely be awful, though there was no doubt it had no sharpness to it.

—*It might be more appropriate to use this more like a cudgel. Just have to make sure I don't hit myself with the blade.*

—*What kind of stats would this have in the game?*

Diablo had most of the weapons memorized since he needed to be able to tell what his challengers were using in the game at a glance. He should especially be able to remember something like this, which looked almost like a joke weapon…

—*I got it!*

Its name in Cross Reverie was the 《Prototype Great Scythe》.

It wasn't something sold in any of the shops. During one of the limited-time events two years ago, there was a lottery you could participate in for prizes—and this weapon was what you got when you lost.

On the Wikis, everyone knew it by its nickname: the "Great (Fail) Scythe."

Looking at the smiling girl before him who he had just given a silver coin to, Diablo felt a little sorry for her.

—For me, at least, I'll make sure to use it as best I can, thought Diablo.

It was the first time in a long while he had changed his equipment. Not to mention this may have been the first time he had picked something by form over function.

Diablo gave the war scythe a few swings.

Noticing this, Rem winced.

"…That is… what you wanted? It's okay as long as you are fine with it, but… How do I put this…"

Alicia made no comment, but Shera happily chimed in.

"You're looking more and more like a bad guy, huh!"

"Ugh… Mhm… I guess you're right…"

Diablo couldn't argue with that; he had just obtained a weapon that raised his "Suspicious" stat through the roof.

†

The Demon Lord's Ring Diablo wore reflected magic; and not just offensive magic his opponents used, but healing spells as well. As such, Diablo had to rely on potions to heal himself.

If he had some friends in the game, he could have someone who specialized in potions make some for him... But because of his Demon Lord role play, he had no allies he could rely on. As a result, Diablo needed to be able to make potions himself, which is why he took the sub-class "Combiner."

—*I was able to use my elemental magic in this world, so the same must go for combining materials as well. I should try and gather some ingredients.*

The item shop—

It was an old building located in a corner of the southern marketplace. Just like the other buildings around it, the walls were made of stones stacked on top of each other. The door to this shop was kept closed as well.

Opening the large door, they stepped inside. There were rows upon rows of shelves lined up, which made everything feel cramped. It was obvious that this shop had way too much inventory, as the shelves were stuffed to the brim with various goods. All sorts of items were here, from things he had seen before, to things he had no idea what they could be. There weren't any names for the items here, let alone descriptions for them.

—*Now that I think about it, less than half the population was literate in the Middle Ages, weren't they.*

If the majority of Adventurers could only read and write their own names, it would be pointless to prepare any kind of written explanations or the like. The only thing in front of each product was a price tag.

"...You have business at the item shop as well?" Rem asked. "Does someone as strong as yourself also have a need for items?"

Shera nodded, agreeing with Rem.

"Yeah, I just can't see you downing a potion or something, you know?"

You needed time and ingredients to make health potions. That's where, when you reached a level where you could finally learn recovery magic in the game, most people would naturally stop using them over time.

Top-rank Adventurers did not rely on items.

—*Well, I guess it is kind of hard to imagine a Demon Lord just guzzling down a potion.*

If you saw the last boss of a game starting to down a potion, it's like... Well, it would ruin their image for one, and break the player's immersion.

Should he protect his image as the Demon Lord, or go for the practical benefits...

He wrestled with it in his head for a second— But he had already come to a conclusion.

If he was defeated because he ran out of potions, even after having all this time to prepare— He would want to die from regret.

First and foremost, he would regret it as a gamer. If anything, he wouldn't be able to protect Shera from the Elves if he was defeated. He would also break his promise to Rem to destroy the Demon Lord Krebskulm sealed inside of her.

If he lost in this world, that was the end. No do-overs.

There were battles here he absolutely needed to win—He couldn't just win by pumping himself up. Only a thorough amount of preparation and exceptional strength would lead him to victory.

Rem and Shera already understood the superiority of Diablo's magic, and Alicia seemed to acknowledge it as well. Even if they saw him buying the ingredients for potions, it shouldn't be enough to deal a fatal blow to his majestic image.

—*...At least, I'm hoping it doesn't.*

Now a bit more faint of heart, Diablo headed deeper into the store.

There, he found an old, beat-up wooden table. Sitting at said table was a girl, reading a book.

—*That's another NPC I remember.*

It was a young Dwarven girl with large, triangular ears, like a chihuahua. Aside from the dog ears and tail, there wasn't much difference between a Dwarf child and a Human child.

When a Dwarven girl reached maturity, her height would still remain on the short side, but their face would become more mature; and her chest would get bigger as well.

In the game, this girl was "a granddaughter watching over the shop while her grandma was away."

Feeling nostalgic, Diablo spoke to her.

"There are some things I need."

"Ah, welcome~ Oh, but, um, grandma isn't back yet... Mmm... Oh well, I guess it's fine. You can buy things, if you want."

It was pretty much the exact same lines from the game.

Apparently, the girl's grandmother never came back in the game; not even once. There were many theories about why this was: there was the "grandma had died on her journey" theory; the "girl was abandoned by the grandma" theory; or the ever-popular, "I'm your grandma now" theory.

It was all just idle chat room banter, with no real answers.

—*But now might be the perfect chance to solve the mystery that's haunted the game for years! You could only buy things from her in-game; but this world is different. I can actually ask her questions here.*

Another, more grave theory had just crossed his mind:

The girl was unable to accept her grandmother's death, and continued to believe her own lies.

If he accidentally overstepped his boundaries and asked too much, he could cause her some kind of deep psychological damage. He wouldn't know what to do next if that happened.

—*Better just stop here. There are some mysteries better left unsolved.*

Diablo listed off the ingredients needed for the 《HP Potion: Beginner》 recipe.

"Do you have 《Forest Poppy Leaves》 and 《Fresh Spring Water》 here?"

The girl put a finger to her lips, as if she were thinking.

"Mm... That we do."

If you combined these two items in the game, you would have yourself a freshly made HP potion.

Diablo suddenly thought of something:

"Do you have anything that can be used as a container for a potion?"

This would be an item that didn't exist in the game. But in this world, there was no way a container would just magically appear when you mixed some herbs and water together.

The shop girl gave the same answer as before—

"Mm... That we do."

—*So there is something like that here...*

On the inside, Diablo breathed a sigh of relief.

If I had forgotten to buy a container after buying all these ingredients to combine them, people would start thinking that I'm clumsy, even though I'm a Demon Lord. I'm just glad that I didn't end up doing something really lame.

"Then I shall take nine of each."

"That's an... odd number to choose."

You could stack nine of the same item in one slot in the game. That's why Diablo had a habit of buying things nine at a time. Although, thinking about it from a more realistic perspective, that did seem a bit weird.

But correcting himself now would just make him look stupid.

"Heh heh heh... There is no possible way for a little girl to understand the meaning behind this amount."

"Mmm... You're right, I don't get it."

"But of course... So, hand over nine of each."

"Okay~"

Leaving her book on the table, the girl trotted around the store. She seemed to have a grasp on where each item Diablo had requested was located amongst the mountains of goods for sale here. In the game, you only had to talk with the merchant and pay them to buy their wares; but in reality, they had to go through the trouble of bringing the items to you.

—*Must be pretty hard for her, running the shop by herself.*

He couldn't help but hope for the girl's grandmother to come back as soon as possible.

After a short while, the girl came back. Carrying a wooden basket, there were nine of each of the forest poppy leaves inside, as well as natural spring water and vials that looked like test tubes.

The poppy leaves were about the size of your palm, and had a fresh, green color to them. The leaves were tied up with string, and the girl removed one from the stack. It seemed that one bundle contained ten leaves, so it must have been fairly rare for a customer to specifically ask for only nine of them.

The water had been measured by eye, and was scooped from a barrel before being moved to leather pouches. One bag seemed to hold about 100 ml of water.

The cylinders that looked like test tubes were apparently called 《Potion Flasks》, and were similar to metallic canteens. They were all stopped off with a cork.

—*For now, that should be enough to test out synthesizing all these together, right?*

To be honest, a beginner HP potion would only heal about 1% of Diablo's total HP. Items all had fixed effects, so once you started leveling up, you would stop noticing the effectiveness of basic items. At the very least, he wanted an advanced HP potion. If he had nine of those, he could make a full recovery even if he was on the verge of death.

For stronger healing potions, or ones that raised stats, there were rare potions that would need even rarer ingredients to make them. In the game, he had maxed out his skills as a Combiner. As long as he had the ingredients, he should be able to make anything. But because he had never tried combining things in this world before, he was nervous about it.

—*I really want an MP potion, though.*

Compared to HP potions, MP potions needed much rarer ingredients in order to make them. But what was it like in this world?

"Do you have 《Kaiser Carrot Roots》 and 《Sacred Mountain Water》 as well?"

The shop girl shook her head.

"Mm... We don't have any rare stuff like that."

"Aren't those materials you can find around here? They should be in the deeper parts of the Man-Eating Forest."

"Mm, you see… You can find them, but it's reeeeeally dangerous, so even if I make a request to the Adventurer's Guild, no one takes the quest."

"Hrm… I see."

Thinking back to the game, there were gathering quests just like this as well. Even if no one took on the quests, there was no way the item shop would ever run out of stock.

But that was that. He didn't even know if he could combine things, and he wasn't about to go out looking for ingredients.

"Give me the total for all this," Diablo announced to the shop-keep.

"Mm… Okie-dokie… Um… Altogether, it's about 9,000 friths."

"That's quite the expense."

Adventurers may be lower-leveled in this world, but the prices for things were quite costly compared to back in the game.

—But that's just how it goes.

In the game, return spells were used everywhere. You could complete gathering quests with only a one-way trip. But even though return magic existed in this world, it was not as widespread. The only things related to it here were legends of Celestials having used it, and rumors that Sorcerers from the Royal Capital could utilize it as well. On top of that, in the game it would take about five to six minutes to get to your destination, as well as a few battles in-between. In this world, however, it would take half a day to make a return trip home, and just a few battles were enough to put your life in danger.

No matter how generous the Adventurer was that gathered these ingredients, they would never sell them for cheap.

Diablo took out three silver coins.

Three silver coins came to 12,000 friths, so he should get 3,000 friths back in change… But that would come out to be 30 copper coins. In times like this, you would often get a silver coin cut in half—a half-silver coin—worth 2,000 friths returned to you.

—Defacing currency like that would be a crime in modern Japan. Must be the easygoing nature of an age without paper money, I guess.

He would get one half-silver coin and ten copper coins back as change.

"Mmm… Then your change is 3,000 friths altogether, dearie."

"Hm."

Her using "dear" when giving him change made her seem like a real grandma's girl. It was kind of like being in some small-town candy shop.

—Now, how should I bring all this back?

It was all fine and dandy that he bought his ingredients, but they were pretty heavy. Carrying all this on top of the Prototype Great Scythe and Tenma's Staff, he was more like a traveling merchant than a Demon Lord.

Alicia stepped forward.

"Shall I carry that for you?"

"Wait. I will try something."

In the game, your item pouch had 30 slots to hold items in. When you first started the game, the pouch only had ten available slots, but you could pay actual money to expand that amount. It was a magic pouch that worked on real money, apparently.

Five slots were 1,500 yen— Basically, it took 6,000 yen to fully unleash the pouch's true potential. That meant spending a lot of real money.

—How's that, my 6,000 yen!?

He tried shoving the leather bags of spring water into the pouch on his waist. Normally, one liter of water would never fit into a pouch just big enough to hold your wallet and cellphone.

Rem, Shera, Alicia, and even the shop girl as well, were all looking at him, mystified.

They smoothly went in.

"Just what I'd expect from 6,000 yen!"

He had said it without thinking. Rem cocked her head to the side and asked, "Is 'Sicks Ow Send En' some kind of spell?"

—Hm? So they don't know what "six thousand yen" means? But they understand "six thousand friths" just fine, though...

Diablo couldn't read the writing of the Lyferian Kingdom himself, yet he was able to talk with others.

—But how does that work?

For starters, I don't even know what language I'm speaking. Everything I've seen from this land makes me think of medieval Europe, so maybe Latin? But this is still another world, though.

He decided to think this over some more later.

Just to be safe, he tried taking the spring water out of the pouch—

No problems there; though it may have looked small on the outside, it felt like the inside was as big as a large backpack— No, it was as wide as a storage room. And when he reached inside, he could feel the item he was aiming for at his fingertips.

—Now this is convenient.

One by one, he stuffed the bundle of poppy leaves and potion flasks in as well. They went in with no problem.

"Whoooooah!?"

The four people watching all exclaimed in surprise.

Rem's voice was trembling.

"…What is that? I have never seen, or even *heard* of a mysterious pouch like that before."

Shera brought her hands together with a **clap**.

"Ah, I know! We had something like that in our treasure vault!"

"Oh hoh? They have something like this in Greenwood as well?"

—*Though I don't think it's because they have a pay-to-play option here.*

"The thing I saw was something called the 《Hundred-Arrow Quiver》, a quiver that you could put a whole bunch of arrows into! When I was a kid, I could only fit 99 in there, though. I was really bummed that I couldn't do the whole one hundred!"

"…A normal quiver can only fit about six arrows at most. I would think that treasure is worth being astounded over," Rem said in amazement.

In Cross Reverie, there was a piece of equipment called a 《Quiver》. It was a container different from the pouch that could hold arrows inside of it. Nine arrows would fill up one spot in your pouch, but a quiver could carry up to 99 of them. Any Archer in the game would be carrying these quivers, but…

"Is it that rare an item?"

"It is~ There's probably only one like it in the entire world, I think."

"Hmm, I see…"

Just about every item in Cross Reverie was also in this world, it seemed. The scarcity of items, however, appeared to be on a whole different level.

"Well, if I can open my own personal treasure vault, I can show you the countless other treasures that are in my possession."

Aside from the pouch, he had used a 《Storage》 in the game. Its capacity was several times larger than the pouch. Even if you lined up every single item implemented in Cross Reverie, there would still be space left over.

Diablo kept a collection of every kind of item in the game, no matter how crappy an item it was.

Since it was a game, there was a handy system that allowed you to take things you had put away in one town's storage and take them out from another town's storage. Not only did he have an abundance of potions stocked up ready to use, if he could take things out of his storage, he would be able to give Rem and Shera equipment equally powerful as his own.

Normally, there would be an individualized counter for each player near the west gate in Faltra, but he hadn't caught sight of it there. There was nothing in the room at the inn, either. This was something similar to teleportation magic, so it might just not exist here.

—Or, maybe… Could it be in my personal area?

Players in Cross Reverie who had gotten above a fixed battle ranking were given a personal area of land to call their own. Fighting over these pieces of land through PvP was one of the features of the game.

Diablo had turned his personal area into a dungeon fitting of a Demon Lord. It was located far, far away from the city of Faltra.

—But it might be good to try going there at least once.

He still couldn't discern what was similar to the game and what was different, but there was a chance that his own dungeon and collection could be in this world as well.

Putting the goods in his pouch, Diablo decided to return to the inn.

†

Leaving the Southern Shopping District, Diablo and his group set out for the "Peace of Mind Inn - Twilight" located along the western road. Diablo was already fairly used to walking amongst the jumble of other races who packed the streets.

—*There were just too many things I was worried about in the beginning here, so I got worn out pretty quickly; but now, dealing with things here is only about as bad as taking a stroll through Akihabara on a day off... Hm? Wait, that's actually still pretty rough...*

It's still light outside, but it must be almost time for dinner.

As they made their way back to the inn, Diablo and the others passed by people like men returning home, and a mother leading her child by the hand.

It was a peaceful scene.

Rem suddenly spoke up in a worried voice.

"...I wonder if it is all right for us to be this relaxed... Though I'm sure this is all part of your carefully laid-out plan, Diablo."

Shera nodded along.

"I just can't seem to calm down... Like, you know, is it all right for me to just be out and about shopping, even though I'm the cause of all this?"

Looking at how peaceful the town was, she probably felt like she was being crushed knowing that a possible war was on the horizon.

But Diablo had nothing at this point. He had some ideas he was thinking about, but no solid plans. Because of that, he was focusing on all sorts of preparation work.

Diablo wanted to make the girls feel a little more at ease, even though he was orally challenged and couldn't speak well to save his life. But if he thought about himself as a Demon Lord, he was able to say things he would normally never be able to say.

"There is no need for you to worry. I said that I would lend you my power, so leave everything to me."

They were words brimming with confidence, and would make him want to die if he said it as his normal self.

A smile crossed Shera's face.

—*That seemed to perk her up a little.*

"Yeah! You're with me, after all! Rem and Alicia, too! There's no way a war is going to happen. I'm different than I was before, scared and living on my own in a dark forest. Now, I've got friends with me!"

Rem made a sour face.

"...It's not like you and I are friends or anything. You just happen to be nearby while Diablo and I are working together."

Her black panther tail swished back and forth restlessly. She must have been hiding her embarrassment behind those words.

Diablo and the girls were all lined up, chatting as they walked. At the front was Diablo; following behind him were Rem and Shera, with Alicia taking up the rear.

It was then that Alicia yelled out:

"What on earth are you doing!?"

Diablo turned around in a panic. Right behind him were the twin Grasswalkers who had attacked them previously at the inn. They had thrown Shera over their shoulders and were forcibly carrying her down the street.

Though they looked like kids, their age was unknown. And if their STR stat was that of a Warrior class, they would be plenty strong.

"Ahh!! L-Let me go!"

Not bothered in the slightest by Shera's screams, they kept on hauling her away.

—To think they'd brazenly attack us in the middle of town like this!

Though she could even detect Elves who had hidden themselves in the forest, Shera couldn't tell if someone held malicious intent for her in this city packed with other beings. Because of that, Alicia had been serving as their lookout and stayed in the back; but it proved impossible to maintain their line when it was this crowded.

It seemed the twins had been waiting for them to be separated by even the tiniest bit.

Alicia drew her sword.

"I am an Imperial Knight! I command you to stop!"

It seemed criminals in this realm were the same as in the real world: not stopping even when they were told to do so. If they could bring Shera back to the Elves, then they'd get her bounty of one billion friths— An amount that would last them a lifetime.

The twins were heading for a cart. If they managed to escape using the cart, it was doubtful that even Diablo could catch up with them.

That being said, he couldn't use magic, either. There were still plenty of townsfolk nearby, and many more who hadn't noticed the turmoil that was unfolding here. They weren't Adventurers, but normal, everyday people. They wouldn't get off with just a few scratches if they were caught up in Diablo's magic. Rem using her Summons was also pretty dangerous.

Diablo set off after the two Grasswalkers.

"Stop them before they reach the cart!"

"Understood!"

Rem and Alicia followed behind him.

Standing in their way was a Dwarf, war axe in hand, and a brawny Pantherian; both of whom were also part of the Adventurers that had attacked them at the inn.

"Whoa, now! Like we'd let you get by!"

"Yer gonna have to play with us fer a while!"

Diablo clicked his tongue.

"Out of the way!"

He swung the war scythe he held in his hands.

—*You better be prepared for a broken bone or two!*

The steel handle bent and warped as Diablo sank the metal into the Pantherian's shoulder with all his might.

With a cracking noise, the Pantherian Brawler's shoulder was broken. He was sent flying, along with the Dwarf who had been standing next to him.

"Gwooooargh!?"

"Whaaaaaaaat!?"

The two assailants fell to the ground in a heap on top of each other, prompting people to actually start backing away. This wasn't the happy-go-lucky kind of world where one could survive after spacing out and watching someone draw their weapons.

The Dwarf and Pantherian managed to wheeze out a few words.

"He's… too strong… Wasn't he supposed to be… a Sorcerer…?"

"Consarn it all…"

While talking, they were managing to stand themselves back up.

—*Guess it's not possible to take them out in one hit, after all.*

Alicia stopped in her place.

"Please, leave them to me!

—*Well, that's thoughtful of her.*

In any case, he had managed to sweep the attackers to the side without killing them. It seemed that the Prototype Great Scythe was a perfect fit for Diablo's STR stat. It wasn't half bad as a weapon to hold himself back.

Taking notice of the disturbance, the townspeople fled to the edges of the street.

Now there was no one to get in his way.

Diablo took off at a full sprint. It was the first time he had unleashed his full potential since coming to this world.

The Ebony Abyss he wore boosted all of his physical abilities, and on top of this, his body was that of a level 150 player. Though he was a Demon Sorcerer, his AGI stat far surpassed that of any of the other races. Like a bike going downhill, each time he kicked off the ground his body moved faster and faster. The surrounding scenery flew behind him.

One of the twins spoke up:

"He's fast, big brother!"

"He is fast, little brother… Maybe he's using a Quickening spell? But, we can make it to the cart before him."

—*I* will *catch up to you!*

Someone emerged from the crowd of onlookers.

A Warrior, clad in golden armor, stood in front of the two twins.

Judging from their body-type, the Warrior looked like a Human. They were wearing a helmet, so Diablo couldn't see their face.

The Warrior drew their longsword.

Flash!

It looked like the tip of their sword had completely disappeared. It was an extremely fast double-strike—the Martial Art 《Double Smash》. It was a technique composed of a slash to the right, then a slash to the left, but unleashed at almost the exact same time.

The twins groaned.

"B-Big brother…"

"Ngh… We were so… close…"

The twins crumpled to the floor, dropping Shera to the ground, butt-first.

"Owie!?"

Diablo had managed to catch up, and was face-to-face with the Warrior clothed in gold.

—*They helped us?*

Either way, that doesn't mean it's a case of "the enemy of my enemy is my friend"— I should stay on guard.

I'll ask for their name first.

"And just who are you?"

"Heh heh heh…" A deep laugh came from the inside of the helmet.

The Warrior in gold revealed his face.

"My dear friend, it seems that I've leveled up so much that you're in shock, aren't you? But of course you would be! My sword and armor were ruined in that fight with the Fallen the other day, so these are all brand new. What do you think of this golden armor! Magnificent, is it not!"

—*So… It's him.*

The Warrior clad in golden armor loudly proclaimed his name:

"My name is Emile Bichelberger! I am an ally to all women, and an ally to those allied to women!"

†

On the boundary between Faltra's Southern and Eastern Districts—

Emile's Adventurer compatriots had restrained the four assailants. The cart they had prepared had been confiscated as well, and they were being gathered to be escorted away.

Never mind that Emile's companions had been close by, or the fact they had the tools and skill to tie someone up; it was as if they had come specifically prepared to capture someone.

"You sure came by at an interesting time. A coincidence?" Diablo asked Emile.

"Oh, this was no coincidence, my friend. I can just *smell* where there are girls in trouble!"

Rem and Shera took about three steps away from Emile.

Alicia was the only one with a smile on her face, staying at Diablo's side.

Diablo let out a sigh.

"Don't do anything that would get you arrested by the Imperial Knights."

"J-Just a joke, of course! Actually, I had heard from the Adventurer's Guild that Prince Keera had placed a bounty on our lovely Shera here."

"A truly foolish affair."

"Kidnapping someone is a grave sin... But the bounty is one billion friths, after all. That's an outrageous amount of money. I thought this might lead to trouble, so my companions and I were out searching for Shera, too."

"Oh hoh? So does that mean you're after the bounty as well, then?"

"Of course not! I am an ally to all women— I would never forgive anyone for doing something that would make Shera sad! I'm here to protect Shera from these misguided fools!"

—*So that's what it was.*

Looks like I can count on Emile after all.

He's the kind of guy who prioritizes protecting girls over his own life.

Diablo nodded.

"Good work out there."

"Heh… I wanted to help you out as my way of saying thanks to you. That potion you gave me was amazing! My wounds were healed in no time at all, and I felt so energized that I didn't even need to sleep for three whole days and nights."

The potion that Diablo gave Emile was one of the best potions in Cross Reverie. Not only did it recover HP and boost one's stats, but it also protected the user from adverse status effects for a fixed period of time. The reason Emile was fine not sleeping was because "Sleep" was a negative status effect in the game.

—Though I think pulling three all-nighters in a row would actually be worse for your health…

It seemed that "a fixed period of time" was much longer in this world compared to the game. The effects of the potion he gave Emile should have lasted for three minutes, at the most. Here, it lasted three days.

—Gathering materials in this world seems to be a lot more troublesome than it is compared to the game… Is that balanced out by having the effects of things here boosted?

Diablo would have to look into that later.

One of Emile's companions, a young man in a white robe, came to tell Emile that they were ready to move the attackers.

"Guess it's about time I round these guys up and get them out of here."

"What are you planning to do with them? This is an attempted kidnapping, and we do have an Imperial Knight right here."

Alicia nodded in agreement, but Emile shook his head.

"Fines and hard labor will not change people. Leave them to me. I have a duty to make all those who would make women cry disappear from this world."

"Are you going to kill them?"

"You sure say some frightening things, don't you… I will drill the message of how important women are into them until they understand it from the bottom of their hearts! We will keep going until they become good and honest people who will not make the mistake of trying to kidnap a woman ever again!"

"Hmph… That sounds like a torture worse than having your body roasted by the flames of purgatory. I shall allow it. Execute them in any way you see fit."

"It's not an execution, but me teaching them the true meaning of love! Now then, I best get going… But there's no guarantee that they're the only people out there blinded by greed because of the bounty. Be careful out there."

Shera ran up to him:

"Thank you, Emile!"

"It's fine, I'm just glad you're safe. Make no mistake, all the Adventurers in this town are your allies."

"Yeah! Tell them I say thanks, too!"

Rem addressed him as well:

"…Not only did you protect me from the Fallen the other day, but now this… I misjudged you, Emile."

Alicia gave a salute.

"The person I was put in charge of protecting was almost abducted. Thank you very much for your assistance."

"Heh heh, no need to thank me!" Emile smiled wide enough to show off his pearly white teeth. "My goodness, yet more girls have become prisoners of love to me! I truly am a man of sin!"

With a boisterous laugh, he headed back towards where his companions were waiting.

As he turned away, the fact that the expressions on the girls' faces darkened at the same time was a truth unknown to him.

Shera tilted her head.

"I think Emile's a good person, but I'm not his prisoner or anything... So who is?"

"...He is not a bad person... But I do not want to be too involved with him, if I can help it," Rem sighed.

"Sigh... This is why men are just... Ugh," Alicia muttered.

Some pretty harsh criticisms came from the girls.

—Well, it's not like a girl will just suddenly fall in love with you because you helped them out a little. Those kinds of situations are just fantasy, after all.

The "pure-hearted maiden" type of girl only existed in games and anime. Diablo had never seen one before in real life.

As if he just remembered something, Diablo beckoned to Shera.

"What is it, Diablo?"

"Do not stray far from me. Stay next to me."

"Huh? Is that all right?"

"It would be troublesome if you were kidnapped again."

"...your... h-hand..."

"Hm?"

"Can I... hold your hand?"

"I see. That way, even amongst crowds of people, it would be harder for someone to come after you. Though there is a possibility they could do something like sever your arm with a single slash..."

"Eek!?"

Shera latched onto his left arm, pressing her chest against him with a *squeeeeze*

113

Diablo's thick arm was buried between two soft, fluffy mounds. He could feel her warmth spreading to him.

"Hrn…"

"U-Um… Thank you for saving me earlier."

"Emile was the one who saved you, was he not?"

"But you were the one who beat up those Grasswalker guys' companions, right? And you had almost caught up to me, too. I was really scared… But then I thought about how you would come save me, and I felt a lot better!"

"…Don't become so placid before you're even saved. You are far too optimistic."

"Ehehe…"

Shera pressed her chest against him again, this time a little more forcibly.

"You're suffocating me."

"But it would be dangerous if I got too far away, riiight?"

"Even so…"

What he was really thinking: "Please, stop sandwiching my arm between your humongous boobs; any sense of reason I have is going to break!"

As they walked, he felt that he was slowly being pulled away from the right side. And on that right side—

This time, Rem was the one who had come up to his shoulder. He was holding the Prototype Great Scythe in his right hand, but she didn't try to wrap around his arm or anything, though.

She touched his shoulder, staring at him with upturned eyes.

"…I was surprised. I had no idea you were that fast."

"Hm? Ah, of course I would be able to do at least that much."

"…I'm sure the Adventurers who attacked us were experts, yet you still overwhelmed them in speed and power. To think that you're that strong, even without using magic... As to be expected of you, Diablo."

"I am not a Sorcerer, but a Demon Lord, after all."

"...Of course."

Rem's eyes were practically sparkling as she stared at him. It seemed she really trusted him.

If he were to blurt something out like, "My magnificence as a Demon Lord has grown again!" then he would be the same as Emile, so Diablo kept his mouth shut.

—*It doesn't really have anything to do with being a Demon Lord, anyways.*

It was just another result of the level gap here. If he was up against a Warrior of the same level in a contest of strength, then there was no way he could win.

For starters, Demons had low STR and AGI stats to begin with. The Ebony Abyss was an extremely rare piece of equipment with superior stats, as well as an ability to raise the wearer's physical abilities; but even so, it only put him on the same level as a level 60 Warrior.

He thought back to Emile's new armor and weapons. From what he could tell, they were just about on the same level; the more Martial Arts Emile had, though, the more it put him at an advantage.

—*Not to mention the difference in experience when fighting against other people.*

You couldn't win with just high stats. You were bound to have a rough time against an opponent who had properly honed their skills as a player. If someone like that appeared, that's when Diablo would use magic. It would be stupid of him to hold back and end up losing because of it.

Further to the right, past Rem, was Alicia. The crowd of people had thinned out, so there was enough room for them to walk in a line.

"Diablo... I apologize for what happened before... I allowed them to attack us from behind, even though I was trusted with guarding the rear... How should I even begin to apologize for such a transgression..."

"You are mistaken."

"What?"

"Do not think that everyone is relying upon you and your power. I am the Demon Lord Diablo... I have never once thought that I needed your help."

In reality, if it wasn't for Alicia's quick-thinking, then the Dwarf and Pantherian attackers from before could have gotten away. Just from the way she moved, he could tell that the sword at her waist was not just for decoration.

But her trying to "be useful to him" was wearing him out.

A hard worker like Alicia was the natural enemy of a lazy person like Diablo. It stimulated his own self-loathing, slowly draining him of his willpower. It would be fine if she was like Rem and accepted herself, or like Shera and relied on him; but hearing Alicia say she would "put even more effort into it" made him want to leave everything to her so he could go back home and sleep.

She probably never had a downer with an apathetic lifestyle like him around her before. Alicia had a bewildered look on her face.

"...Th-Then...just how exactly should I prove myself useful to you?"

"Are you one of those types of people? The kind who thinks that those who don't serve a purpose should die?"

"What!? That, that isn't... It is not like that at all!"

She denied it much more strongly than he had expected. But maybe that was to be expected from an Imperial Knight charged with protecting the weak.

"Then you need to forgive yourself, even if you aren't useful to me. If you wish to accompany us, then do as you please. You do not even have to try and bring about results, either."

"Y-Yes…"

He had hoped that he would have been able to put Alicia at ease, but because of his chronic foot-in-mouth disorder, he had made her face turn pale instead.

—*Is that so hard to accept for a goody-two shoes like her, who's done nothing but constantly endeavoring to be her best?*

But Diablo was doing things at his own pace. To have someone right next to him attempting to bring out her very best, it was as if she was trying to push the boundaries of the human race… It was a lot for Diablo to take in, to be frank.

If he were to keep focused on the quest at hand, he wanted Alicia to conduct herself in a slower-paced manner. He wasn't sure if he had gotten the point across or not, but…

"I understand." Alicia nodded. "I will endeavor to do my absolute best to forgive myself, even if I cannot be of use to you."

—*Well that didn't work at all…*

†

It was still a little too early for dinner at the dining hall of the "Peace of Mind Inn - Twilight." Only three customers were to be found here.

Diablo had already become completely accustomed with this place. Though the people here had been suspicious of him at first, after showing up here a few times, they stopped being startled by his appearance. In fact, it had gotten to the point you could tell a person wasn't a regular at this dining hall if they were shocked at seeing Diablo.

But today, even the regulars here did a double-take when they saw him.

The reason: the Prototype Great Scythe he held in his hands.

Diablo walked through the town, but there was no one who had a weapon as ominous and sinister-looking as his.

—I'm sure they'll get used to it after a few days.

While attracting stares from all around him, Diablo settled down at the round table he always used. Rem and Shera were sitting on either side of him with Alicia sitting directly across from Diablo.

The receptionist and poster girl of the inn—the Pantherian, Mei—came over to them. She had brown hair that came down to her shoulders, and a bright, cheerful smile on her face. She was wearing a frilly uniform that made you wonder if it was supposed to be for a maid or an idol.

"Welcome, welcome, welcome! ♪"

"Hm."

"Ah, before I get your order— The wall of the room you're all using is being fixed right now; but you're still staying tonight, right?"

"That was my intention."

"I apologize for all the trouble we caused," Rem said, bowing her head as she apologized. Shera, likewise, bowed.

Alicia did not know what they were talking about, and so remained silent.

The idol of the inn waved her hand dismissively.

"It's fine, it's fine! I'm already used to Adventurers causing trouble, so don't you worry about li'l ol' me~ ♪ Ah, but I'm gonna have to ask you for this much, though! Kyaha~ ☆"

She laid a piece of paper down on the table with an almost revolting amount of money listed for the repair bill.

—*Holy crap, are you planning on completely rebuilding that room or something!?*

Just because she was smiling, it didn't mean that she was going to go easy on them.

It was survival of the fittest here in another world.

It was an amount that Diablo and the others couldn't hope to pay, so he privately decided to have the assailants from earlier take care of it. They were the ones to break the wall, after all.

As if nothing had happened, Mei took their orders.

"I recommend the 'Mei Special' today! ♪"

"Then we shall have that."

"Four of them, please," Rem added.

In almost no time, the food was brought out to them:

Potatoes; sausages; hard-baked bread; clear soup with boiled vegetables similar to eggplant and cabbage; and a wooden tankard full of water.

Diablo had been in love with the sausages here ever since the first day he had tried them—so much so that he ate one a day.

Today, as always, he went for the sausages first. It had a nice, crispy chewiness as he bit into it. The next instant, he was overcome with a dynamic combination of the flavor of meat and the soft fragrance of herbs as it spread throughout his mouth. As he chewed, he could feel the coarse texture of the meat; each time he bit down, his mouth was flooded with its savory juices. It was also flavored with salt, packing quite a punch.

Diablo tore off a piece of bread and popped it in his mouth. It had a hard, crunchy texture, with no flavor. But when it was combined with the salt flavor, the fragrance of the herbs, and the juiciness of the sausage, the delectability of it all was increased several-fold.

Relishing these flavors until they faded from his mouth, Diablo took a slow, long drink of water.

Another delicious meal.

Looking to his right, he saw Rem eating her meal in a very refined manner. But when he looked to his left—

Shera hadn't touched her food.

Diablo wasn't good at showing concern for other people in times like this. If he were to coerce her, she would probably have even less of an appetite.

"Miss Shera, it seems you have barely touched your food. Is something the matter?" Alicia asked in a gentle voice.

With a jump, Shera came back to reality.

"U-Uh, it's nothing! I was just, um, spacing out... Maybe I'm just tired or something? Ahaha…"

With a forced laugh, she pretended she was all right.

—*So, she really is torn up about this... But of course she would be. Anyone would if they were the cause of a war almost breaking out.*

Because of the flurry of activity that had been happening around her, she was able to keep up her usual cheerfulness. But now, taking their time as they ate—

It must have been weighing heavy on her mind.

Alicia spoke in a caring manner:

"If you do not eat, it will only harm your body. Now more than ever do you need to make sure to keep up your physical strength. Please, if only just a little, try and eat something."

"Yeah... You're right. It would be rude to Mei if I just left it. I'm gonna eat!"

She let out a loud voice, as if she were pumping herself up, then bit into one of the sausages. Though slow, Shera started to eat.

Seeing that, Diablo breathed a silent sigh of relief.

†

They continued eating in silence for a while. The other customers from before had already left, so Diablo and the others were the only ones remaining, though there was sure to be more coming for dinner, soon enough.

Suddenly—

Alicia and Shera both flinched, reacting to something.

—*It's not more attackers, is it?*

Diablo put down the bread he was holding and reached for his war scythe that was leaning against the wall.

The receptionist appeared.

"Reeeem! You have a guest. ☆"

Following Mei in quick succession were people all wearing familiar outfits. They were the brown robes that were the uniform of the Mage's Association. Six of them entered, making the already small dining hall feel even smaller.

And last, in came a single woman—

A woman they knew.

She was beautiful, with a gentle air about her. Her hair came down well below her waist, and she held a long staff in her hand, proof that she was a Sorcerer herself. Her outfit, on the other hand, didn't expose much of her skin, but it fit well enough to show off the sensual curves of her body, making it hard to know where it was okay to look.

A gentle smile on her face, she looked at Diablo with her ice-blue eyes.

"Diablo, Rem, Shera— It's been quite a while, hasn't it."

It was the head of the Mage's Association: Celestine Baudelaire.

Aside from Diablo, she was the only other person who knew that the soul of the Demon Lord Krebskulm was sealed inside of Rem.

Besides the six Sorcerers who had entered before Celes, there were four more guards who had formed a circle around her; but she only had two of them before, though.

"This seems fairly severe, don't you think, Celes?"

"I'm sorry… Despite everyone here, this is the amount only after I had them reduce the number of guards at my side. The elders are still very worried."

The other day, Celes had almost been killed by the Fallen. If she were to die, the barrier protecting the town from monsters and other Fallen would disappear.

Because of this, Faltra had been in danger of falling to the enemy.

—*Actually, it's amazing they let her be outside at all.*

Alicia stood up from her seat and gave a salute.

"A pleasure to make your acquaintance. I am Alicia Cristela, Imperial Knight."

"My, my. I am Celestine Baudelaire, head of the Mage's Association of this town. Very nice to meet you."

—Seeing people act so polite to Celes makes me realize again just how much of an important person she is.

Rem stood up and spoke:

"…Celes, first how about having a seat?"

"I wouldn't be a bother to you, would I?"

"…I cannot keep calm if you are going to stay standing up like that."

"Ahah, I see. My apologies."

Alicia offered her seat.

"Lady Baudelaire, I apologize this is a table we're in the middle of using for dinner. I shall take my leave momentarily, so would you care to use this seat?"

"Oh no, it's fine. How about I borrow one of those chairs from next to you? Oh, but would that be too cramped? Ah, perhaps I should leave and wait until you're all finished eating?"

"Perish the thought! Lady Baudelaire, that simply will not do!"

In a panic, Alicia tried to stop her.

Diablo shrugged his shoulders, letting out a sigh.

"Alicia, bring over one of those chairs. Celes, you will sit there."

He didn't want to end up being the target of another one-sided hatred from a different psycho member of the Mage's Association for making their leader wait outside.

A chair was prepared right away, and Celes sat between Alicia and Rem.

The after-meal coffee was brought out, with one for Celes as well.

There was an exchange of greetings, and as they say: the more girls there were, the louder things became.

Celes bent forward, fixing her eyes on Shera.

"Shera, I heard about what's happening. Cheer up, OK? Just seeing your enthusiastic self makes me very happy."

Shera's eyes went wide.

"You think I'm enthusiastic?"

"Yes, of course. You're so free, after all. That's a wonderful thing. I chose this way of living, so it might cause trouble for me to say this... But I'm a fan of yours, you know?"

"Huh...? I don't really get it, but... Ehehe...! Thanks!"

The enormous ritual magic that enveloped Faltra could not be performed by any normal Sorcerer, but only a chosen genius. For Celes, it seemed she wouldn't be able to leave Faltra until she was old enough and forced to retire—or until she passed away.

It wasn't that she was being forced to do this; she chose a life as the head of the Mage's Association.

Those who dedicated their lives to their work were not particularly a rare sight. Diablo didn't think of them as being especially unfortunate, either. But he could still understand why Celes would want to cheer on Shera in her pursuit of a life of freedom.

As if she had received those feelings, Shera raised both her hands in the air.

"Alrighty! I'm gonna do my best! I'm all better now, and I'm gonna give it my all! With gusto!!"

With the usual smile on her face, she sounded like her normal self again.

—*Did that lift her spirits a little? Gotta be thankful to Celes for that one, then.*

Celes turned to speak to Diablo.

—*So, now we're getting down to business.*

"Today, I have three things I wish to talk with you about, Diablo."

If she only wanted to talk, then a letter or something would have sufficed. Celes not wanting to use her authority for these kinds of things was both one of her good points, and one of the more troublesome things about her.

Diablo nodded.

"Speak, I shall allow it."

Celes smiled with her eyes.

"First, let me thank you once again for saving all of us from the Fallen who invaded the other day."

Celes deeply bowed her head; the guards around her also took a knee as a sign of respect.

Diablo grit his teeth to hide his embarrassment.

"...Make no mistake, it was only because that Fallen was an eyesore..."

"Even so, your actions protected the city of Faltra from falling to the enemy. Normally, this would be a feat that would earn you a few words from His Majesty himself. However—"

As if it were hard to say, she averted her eyes.

Diablo shook his head.

"I have no need for anything as contrived as that."

Humans were the race who should be opposing the Fallen. Especially in this Human-built Kingdom, it was Humans themselves who held most of the power and authority here.

Demis were discriminated against. Demons like Diablo were especially shunned, due to their similarities to the Fallen. The town most likely did not want to praise a Demon hero. On top of that, Diablo had ominous horns growing out of his head; called himself a Demon Lord; and was an Elemental Sorcerer, which was claimed to be one of the weakest vocations in this world.

Basically, there were too many reasons for these big-shots to not want to commend his efforts.

Celes bowed her head apologetically.

"I extend my apologies on this matter."

"I told you, I have no need for it. I am not partial to things that would draw attention to me."

In this country that held Demis in contempt, even if he became close to the people in power, it seemed that it would only cause more trouble. There were still plenty of things he wanted to try in this world. The life of a carefree Adventurer definitely suited him the most.

"There are so many people out there, myself included, who are grateful toward you... I just wanted you to know that."

"Hm."

"If you should ever need something, I am available to do anything on your behalf."

—Hm? She just said she would do... anything?

Diablo almost reacted to this, but played it off by coughing instead.

"It is inconceivable to think there will ever be a time I should require your help! That being said, I have received your intentions. That should be enough for you, correct?"

"Yes, of course."

An expression of relief crossed Celes's face.

"...You truly did defeat Gregore by yourself," Alicia muttered.

"Oh? So you still did not believe it."

"Oh, no... I was aware of it from the information I was given, but... Even amongst the other Fallen, Gregore was considerably strong... It was difficult to believe it myself."

"You would call that thing 'strong'?"

"The strongest Sorcerer in the Man-Eating Forest."

"You sure are knowledgeable about this, aren't you?"

A smile crossed Alicia's lips.

"I appreciate that… The biggest threat to Faltra is not the Kingdom of Greenwood, but the Fallen. I have thoroughly and repeatedly poured over the reports myself. Even in the past, it has been recorded that the Fallen known as 'Gregore' was known as a being of significant power. Hearing that someone had defeated him single-handedly… I had planned on coming to terms with that after seeing you… But it is a different kind of shock, hearing it again like this."

—Like a true honors student, it seems she knows of what I did, but only took it as a piece of intel… She didn't actually believe it until now. But after hearing what Celes had to say, I guess she was finally convinced.

Alicia's intuitions are pretty plain after all…

Well, I guess it would be normal to find this all hard to believe, huh.

It seemed that those who had never seen Diablo fight wouldn't believe how strong he was.

Diablo had decided not to worry about it. He hadn't been fighting so that others would accept how strong he was; back then, he was fighting because he wanted to save Rem and Celes. Not only that, but he couldn't forgive that Fallen for killing all the people he did. Words should be met by words, and force should be met by force. If his opponent was ready to kill, Diablo would not hold back.

Satisfied, Diablo prompted for Celes to continue.

Celes listed off her second order of business:

"I thought it would be good to explain where the Mage's Association stands regarding the matter with the Kingdom of Greenwood."

Diablo certainly couldn't ignore the strength of the Mage's Association. It was necessary for him to have an understanding of what they would do, and he couldn't imagine Celes actively wanting a war with the Elves— But this was a situation where they would be forced to make a move.

She continued to speak:

"The Mage's Association holds part of the burden when it comes to the protection of Faltra. That's why when something poses a threat to this town, we will cooperate with the army. And because I am not used to combat or fighting, I believe the governor will be entrusted with command over everyone."

—Tch.

So that means when the governor goes to mobilize the army, the Mage's Association will be there alongside them...

Judging by the expression on Celes's face, he could tell that not only did she not wish to go war, but she was distressed about having other members of the Mage's Association be given orders by the governor to fight.

Diablo didn't want to get them involved. To do that, he was trying to create a situation where the governor would not have to mobilize the army. The essential thing here was to avoid this war.

Diablo finished off the rest of his now cold coffee.

"I have already accepted a request to avoid war with the Kingdom of Greenwood. The Mage's Association will have no part to play in this; I will see to it these Elves do not show up before the city of Faltra."

"Thank you... Hearing you say that is a great relief to me."

Celes wiped tears from the corners of her eyes.

—*She's really expecting a lot from me. Though in reality, I'm still only in the middle of thinking over how to avoid this war.*

"This is the last order of business," Celes said, laying an envelope on the table.

"What is this?" Diablo asked, glancing at it.

"Something that may become a lead to removing the Enslavement Collars."

"Oh hoh?"

He couldn't help but be surprised at this.

"…What do you mean?" Rem reacted inquisitively.

"It's only a possibility, so I don't want to get your hopes up too much… Right now, there is a slave trader caravan at the Central Plaza. The fundamentals for Slave Collars and Enslavement Collars are the same, magic-wise, so…"

"…I see. They may be able to tell us something, then," Rem said, staring at the envelope.

"Enslavement collars" were meant to be put on Summons, while "slave collars" were meant to be put on actual slaves. In this world, if a collar was placed on anyone here, regardless of race, it seemed they would be thought of as slaves.

According to what Celes had said, both collars seemed to be the same fundamentally.

Slaves and slave traders didn't exist in Cross Reverie, so Diablo didn't know much about it… But it sounded like the traders would know the most about how to handle slave collars. They might be able to remove the collars from Rem and Shera.

"Is that envelope a letter of introduction?" Diablo asked to confirm.

"Yes. You can't enter the slave emporium without one... On top of that, I have requested they provide you information as a Sorcerer, not a customer."

"I see... Then I shall make a trip there now."

Though he was in the middle of wondering what to do about the Kingdom of Greenwood, if they could get these collars removed, he wanted to do it as soon as possible.

"It's located on the eastern side of the Central Plaza... It's quite a large purple tent, so you'll know it as soon as you see it."

Rem expressed her gratitude to Celes.

Shera, who was usually fairly clueless about these things, had also managed to follow along with the conversation.

"You mean we can get these collars off!? Thanks, Celes!"

"It's only a possibility... But I'm praying for it to happen."

Diablo grabbed the envelope off the table.

—*I'm a little worried since I can't read what this says... But, it's not like I'm reading this out loud, so it should be fine.*

"...So... We might be able to remove these," Rem murmured.

"I've gotten kinda used to it now, so it feels like it'd be all breezy if it wasn't there anymore," Shera said with a smile.

"Nooo thank you! It's really hard to wash your neck with this thing on, you know!"

"...I will not deny that, but that is not the main problem here."

—*It seems like they've gotten used to life with those collars on. I gotta hurry up and get those off of them,* Diablo thought to himself.

†

The Central Plaza—

It was the largest plaza in Faltra, located on the southern side of the Central District where the governor and all the other fancy-pants aristocrats lived. There were numerous food stands and street vendors open at this time, and the streets were flooded with people, making everything feel a bit cramped.

Celes had left, so it was just Diablo, Rem, Shera, and Alicia now as they reached the place Celes had told them about previously.

It was a large purple tent at the eastern part of the Central Plaza with a soldier standing at the entrance. Unlike the other soldiers and Adventurers, he kept an orderly personal appearance, and wore armor that was different from the regular soldiers. In other words, he was a hired guard.

As they approached, he raised his hand.

"Do you have a referral?"

He was fairly polite for a soldier. He didn't even look at Diablo like he was some kind of freak.

Diablo showed him the letter of invitation.

"...Oh? A referral from the head of this town's Mage's Association is quite rare... Actually, it might be the first time this has happened. Welcome, to 《The Beloved Traveler》."

That seemed to be the name of this slave emporium.

Diablo and the others entered the tent. There were cloth partitions on the inside along a thin pathway, and the scent of orchids drifted throughout the air.

There were two customers here ahead of them; a man and a woman from what Diablo could see, both of whom seemed to be quite affluent people. If people like them were here as customers, the prices for slaves had to be steep.

The design of the shop was similar to an aquarium or a pet shop with cages lined up facing the pathway. But it wasn't animals inside the cages— Other races were held captive there.

Dwarves, Pantherians, Grasswalkers... He didn't see any Demons or Humans, but they were probably around here somewhere.

There were plenty of adults, but there were some that looked like children as well. They were simply dressed, but the clothes they wore were surprisingly neat and tidy. They all sat on chairs inside their cages.

Seeing Diablo and the others, they offered the group amiable smiles. Some of them had smiles that were stiffer than the others.

—I guess that's what you'd call a "business smile"...

So this is a slave emporium...

For the most part, it was exactly like he imagined it would be, but something felt a bit off to him. The equipment and fixtures being used definitely fit the bill, but the slaves themselves were different from the images he had in his head. He had steeled himself for a sea of dead eyes, and people on the verge of madness...

Instead, the place emanated a much more peaceful and gentle impression. In a way, the people who were made to carry heavy luggage around town looked like they had it rougher. The stall vendors who didn't get many customers had more lifeless eyes than the slaves here.

The customers here weren't like the scum you would see in snuff scenes of similar situations, but rather an older couple who were looking to find a pet to keep in their golden years together.

"Are all slave emporiums similar to venues like this?" Diablo asked Rem.

"...This is my first time actually seeing one... I do not know if this one is an exception, or if all the others are like this as well."

"Yeah, same goes for me, too."

"And I as well. However, one of my colleagues had arrested a slave trader for excessively cruel treatment…"

Passing through the hanging cloth that led to the deeper part of the tent, an extraordinarily beautiful woman appeared along the pathway.

—*A Human, huh.*

She was wearing a purple cocktail dress with a deep slit that left her shoulders uncovered, and the area around her chest remarkably exposed. She seemed to be older than Diablo, but just looking at the smoothness of her skin was enough to make you wonder if she was in her late teens. Her high heels clicking against the floor, she walked towards them.

Trying not to stare at her chest took a Herculean effort.

She opened her crimson-colored lips as she came up right in front of them

"Oh my, how lovely. I'd be willing to pay quite a handsome price for either one of those wonderful girls of yours."

"This is no joking matter!"

"How rude of me. I am the owner of this establishment, Medios. You brought two slaves in with you, so I assumed you were here to sell—"

As she was talking, she turned to look behind Diablo, cutting the conversation short with a sharp gaze.

As if she had been overwhelmed, Alicia froze up.

"Do you… need something from me?"

"I am a respectable merchant, you know. I do not believe I have conducted any business that would require the intervention of an Imperial Knight."

Similar to the police, getting a visit from an Imperial Knight was likely a wholly unexpected surprise. And it was true that, despite all the cages and slaves, the atmosphere of the place wasn't completely distasteful.

Alicia bowed her head.

"My sincerest apologies. While I am indeed an Imperial Knight, I have not come here because of any suspicions toward this slave emporium… If I am a bother, I shall wait outside."

Medios craned her neck, skeptically.

"Is that true?"

"You can just think of me as a kind of escort."

"An escort? I do believe this Demon wouldn't need such a thing, though…?"

She spoke as if she knew the true extent of Diablo's power.

"Have you heard something about me?"

"Oh, no. I don't even know your name. But just by looking at your magic energy's flow, I can tell you are no ordinary person… Enough that if I had multiple lives, it wouldn't even be enough to survive rousing your anger."

"The flow of magic energy?"

Diablo couldn't perceive anything of the sort. Thinking back to the level measurement he took at the Adventurer's Guild, there was no one who could sense "the flow of magic energy" or anything like that. Presumably even Sylvie wouldn't be able to see it.

—*Is it just a bluff?*

Getting excited, Shera spoke up.

"I know, right! You can tell Diablo is strong with just one look at him!"

"Oh my, my, my! Can you, too, see the flow of magical energy? You might be more suited to be a trader, rather than a slave."

Medios spread her arms, the air warping and twisting around her.

"Yeah! There's a bunch of light gathering there!" Shera said, still excited.

"Precisely! It seems you really are able to observe it."

"So you really *can* see the flow of magic, too! Even when I told people about it, nobody believed me… I thought I was the only one being a weirdo or something!"

—*Shera can see it, too!?*

Rem shrugged her shoulders.

"…I haven't a clue what they are talking about… I have never seen this 'flow' that Shera mentioned."

Alicia shook her head.

"I've no talent whatsoever as a Sorcerer, so I do not know either."

Medios rhythmically moved her hands closer together and farther apart, the flow of magic energy occurring there only visible to her and Shera.

"Hehehe… This is the result of grueling and painstaking discipline."

"…If you train, then you can see them?"

Medios nodded in response to Rem's inquiry.

"I was able to visualize it three days sooner than Celestine. She was superior to me in every way… But there are occasions where effort exceeds talent!"

"…I… I see."

"Huh? I've been able to see them ever since I was a kid, though…" Shera mumbled to herself.

Everyone went silent.

—*Looks like this whole time I've had a genius nearby.*

Getting a hold of herself, Medios begin to speak once more:

"Well... By any means, if the master issues a command using the collar, then you can notice magic energy there. Not being able to see that, however, makes being a slave trader all the more difficult."

"You can see the commands?"

"Of course, and that's why I find you all so strange. Even though these two are your slaves, you haven't given them any commands."

"These two are not my slaves."

Diablo produced the envelope from Celes. Taking it, Medios used her long nails as a paper knife to open it.

She read the letter inside. Diablo was unable to read the language of this world, so he had no idea what the contents of the letter could be.

Medios smiled wide, showing off her canines.

"I see, I see... I thought it curious for someone on the straight and narrow like Celestine to introduce customers to such an establishment. So I just have to disclose the method to remove the Enslavement Collars, correct?"

"Can you do it?"

"Now, I wonder... This is the first time I've faced a special situation like this. If you ask whether it's possible or not, I would hesitate to give an answer. But it's worth giving it a try, don't you think?"

Medios turned her gaze towards Shera. Then, she looked at Rem.

Medios wore an apprehensive expression.

"Hm? Now you have an interesting magic flow, don't you? Why is magic constantly radiating out from you, I wonder... Are you using some kind of spell? No, this feels like something different..."

"...Wh-What is it?"

"You… Do you have any recollection of being pregnant with a Demon?"

"Th-This is no time for jokes!"

"Whaaaaaat!?" Shera flared up at the now red-faced Rem. "No fair! When did this happen!?"

"Wh-What kind of drivel are you spouting now, Shera!? We have been together almost the entire time! Though you and Diablo have had time alone, too, haven't you!?"

"Aha! Back when he was torturing you! That's when you and him—"

"W-We did not do anything of the sort!"

"But if two people sleep together by themselves in the same bed, that's how you make a baby, right!?"

Everything fell silent.

Blushing madly, Rem lowered her gaze.

"…You can rest assured, that is no way to make children. Not to mention Diablo is a Demon, while I am a Pantherian, so we cannot fathom having offspring together. The same goes for an Elf like yourself, Shera."

"Oh. OK, then!"

Medios, having started this whole exchange, tilted her head to the side.

"Mhm, that is correct. Then the reason I sense the presence of a Fallen from a Pantherian must be…"

"Ngh!?"

Rem grabbed her stomach and backed away.

—Bad! This is really bad!

The soul of the Demon Lord Krebskulm was sealed inside of Rem. Diablo wanted to avoid letting anyone know of her situation at all costs.

He raised his voice:

"Cease this pointless chatter! Are you going to tell me how to remove these collars or not!?"

Medios spread her arms wide in a placating manner.

"Oh my, how rude of me. Celestine is the one who referred you, so of course I will tell you. We studied under the same master, after all. We're almost like sisters."

—Ah, I get it now. I was wondering how someone like Celes was connected to a slave trader.

Magic was a necessity for a slave trader. Not only that, they needed to be highly skilled in using it.

—So, they both studied at the Mage's Association together... One eventually became the leader of the Association, and the other, a slave trader.

"I am not a fan of absurd chatter. You shall tell me now."

"Of course, but understand I treat this matter as a 'trade secret.' We can't speak here, and I would like to keep the number of people I tell this to as small as possible. Come this way... But only those whom this concerns."

She beckoned towards the deeper part of the pathway.

Alicia gave a quick salute.

"Then I shall stay on standby outside."

Rem stepped away.

"...I will pass, too. I do not feel so well, so I wish to rest outside..."

—I was planning to rely on Rem's knowledge of magic for this, to be honest...

But there was a chance this stranger could find out about the Demon Lord's soul, so of course she would be scared. This wasn't the benevolent Celes, but a slave trader. It was only natural that Rem wouldn't want Medios to know her secret.

"Are you OK, Rem?" Shera asked, concerned. "You don't look so good… Do you need to go to the doctor?"

"…Were you able to see the magic coming from me as well?"

"Huh? Oh, yeah, sometimes. I always thought it was because you were a really strong Adventurer… Diablo is way stronger, though."

"I see…"

"What's up?"

"…I'm glad that you are an idiot, Shera."

"That's so mean!!"

Diablo reached out and grabbed Shera by the sleeve.

"Leave her. She'll get better if she rests. We have no time to waste; we're going."

"Waaaah! Stop it, Diablo! It's stretching! You're stretching out my clothes!! If you're going to pull, then at least do it from my collar!"

"*That's* what you're fine with!?"

†

They moved to a different tent, away from the main exhibit where all the slaves were on display. Inside this smaller tent was a large bed with a mattress filled with cotton; it wasn't one of the crude ones that just had some sheets thrown over a bit of straw. There was also a table, with four chairs gathered around it.

If this was supposed to be the private room of a slave trader, it was odd there was no desk. On the other hand, if it was supposed to be a reception office, it was strange for a bed to even be here. It was a peculiar room all around.

Sitting in one of the chairs, Medios crossed her shapely legs. She lit up a long metal pipe.

"Now then... Diablo and Shera, was it? Have a seat wherever you would like."

"That was my first time seeing a slave emporium!" Shera exclaimed excitedly.

"Hehe, is that so. How was it?"

"It was a lot less horrible than I thought it would be!"

Diablo felt the same; whenever he heard "slave emporium," the images that circulated in his mind were much more gruesome. But even though the slaves here were indeed inside cages, they did not seem so badly off.

Medios spoke as she laughed.

"Ahahaha! I would certainly hope so! Suppose you were to come looking to buy a slave, Shera. Would you want one that was suffering from illness? Or one whose eyes looked like they had lost all hope?"

"Nope, I don't think I would."

"And that is precisely my point. Smithies display their wares after they have been polished; item shops gather their goods and put them on display. Keeping our slaves' minds and bodies clean is only natural for a slave emporium."

It made sense. Because all the slaves looked healthy and fit, this made it easier to feel relieved when purchasing them.

—*Not that I'm gonna buy a slave or anything, though.*

Medios continued:

"I would say it also has to do with who I am as a person. Though I may not look it, I am quite the pushover. If any one of my slaves is suffering, then I want to help them, and I want to teach them how to make their masters happy before they are bought. I think of them all as my children, so there's no way I could treat them horribly."

"Oh, I got it! So you're a really good person, Medios!"

"…Even though I am a slave trader?"

Medios laughed again.

Taking a puff from her pipe, Medios stood up from her chair.

"Very well, shall I teach you, then? Practice above theory! After all, there exist no theories regarding a situation so unique as yours."

"I shall—"

He had started to say "I shall allow it, so tell me," but he stopped himself. Just this once, he thought that making this a success should be his priority.

Diablo opened his mouth.

"…If you would."

"Oh yes, that way suits you much better."

Diablo turned his gaze away from Medios's grin.

She gave an order to Shera.

"All right, strip."

"Huh?"

"I'm going to use you to teach Diablo how to use 《Enslavement Magic》. Though you may have a grasp on the flow of magic, those enchanted clothes of yours will only get in the way."

"What? But these are just some normal clothes with a bit of magic flowing through it."

Medios touched the fabric with her fingers.

"…Normal clothes usually don't have magic flowing through them."

"Well, I guess you're right. B-But, being naked is embarrassing… And Diablo is watching, too…"

141

"Hm? Aren't you two in that kind of relationship?"

Shera tilted her head, confused.

Diablo clamped down on his back teeth to prevent himself from blushing.

"Can we not use other clothes?"

"That's fine, but the only extra clothes I have… Let's say they aren't normal."

Shera sat on the bed, squirming in embarrassment. The outfit she wore looked like some kind of lingerie. Since it barely covered anything, it was hard to tell if it was made of cloth or simply strings. There were also beads dangling over one of the more… private places of the outfit.

—*Just what are the point of those beads!?*

As if admiring her own handiwork, Medios nodded.

"This is an outfit for sex slaves, but it suits you quite nicely."

"Weren't they supposed to be your children!?"

Without thinking, Diablo fired back this retort.

Medios puffed her chest out proudly.

"All is fair when it comes to business! They won't be able to survive unless they accept that, so that is what I teach them. If you say that you can save all the poor and needy right now, then I will apologize for being wrong, though."

"Tch… You sure have a way with words, don't you. You're completely different from Celes. …Fine. Now, what should I do?"

"All right, now start by touching Shera's skin. Anywhere is fine, but I would say her torso would be much better than her arms or legs."

—*Easier said than done, lady.*

Diablo climbed on top of the bed where Shera was waiting. His hands were shaking, even though it wasn't his first time touching her body...

—*Well, it is the first time that it's not over her clothes, though...*

For now, he laid his hand on her collarbone.

"Mm..."

Shera's body twisted, as if this was tickling her.

"Don't make strange noises like that."

"B-But... Your hand..."

Medios called out away from the bed.

"Pardon me, you two? It's a little too early to start setting the mood like that, don't you think? Now then, Diablo, try getting a read on her magic."

"Ngh... That's pretty sudden."

"If you can manipulate magic, you can do this. Even if you cannot perceive it, the ability to experience it should be a piece of cake."

When she said it like that, it must have been similar to the feeling you get from using magic.

Rather than touching skin, he tried thinking of it as if he was using his staff. It was then he felt something flowing inside of her. It was different from the blood that ran throughout her body. It twisted all around her, originating from her heart and working its way down to the lower part of her stomach.

And then, the flow that was around Shera's neck...

—*Is this it!?*

"Ngh... It's gone?"

The magic's sensation suddenly disappeared from his fingertips.

"Magical energy is something you are unable to see when you want to see it, and when you try to sense it, you will not. That means you have to feel it without *trying* to feel it," Medios explained.

—*Like I said, way easier said than done, lady.*

"Now, how about we investigate an area where the magic energy is a bit more focused, then."

"So, there's a place like that. That's something you should have said from the beginning."

"If you felt it, if only for an instant… I would believe you have come to realize the answer, no?"

"It went from the heart… and then downwards."

"Correct, so start there! Once you can begin feeling the magic energy, I'll begin my lecture on enslavement magic."

—*So you're saying I haven't even made it to the starting line yet?*

Diablo leaned himself over Shera. He didn't have time to take things slow and steady.

"Here I come, Shera… Prepare yourself."

"Y-Yeah… Diablo… This is kind of… scary…"

"Just leave everything to me."

—*I'm going to learn this magic and get those collars off!*

Just as Medios had ordered, he reached out and placed his hand over Shera's heart. His fingers sank into her soft chest. The almost non-existent fabric provided no interference at all.

Shera gave a soft moan.

"Fwaaa…"

"Guh… It's still too far away."

He tried pushing upwards. The fabric on her chest seemed like it was going to fall away.

But he could feel the flow of the magic energy.

"Mm... Dia—ahh, if... if you do it that strongly... Nng... I think that's... one of my weak spots... so... Mm!"

"Endure it. This is where the magic is gathering."

He rubbed her all over with his hands, changing his position along the way. It also transformed the way he saw things. He had begun to visualize a more three-dimensional image of how the magic energy flowed.

"Nnng! Ahhn! Ah! Ah! You... nng, you can't... do that... Haa!"

"Just a little more!"

"Ah! Aaah! But if you do it... a little more... then, I'm... I'm going to...!"

Medios started giving instructions:

"It seems you've begun to see it. Then let's try heading downwards a bit more, shall we? This time, you will insert some of your own magic energy there. The procedure for applying this magic begins by attaining a firm grasp of the magic energy. Then, your aim is to directly interfere with said energy. Finally, you solidify the interference and supply it a fixed shape—"

As he listened, Diablo started sliding his hands. It felt like if he took his hands away, he wouldn't be able to find it again.

Shera's skin felt smoother and softer than anything he had felt before in his life. The sensation spread to the deepest parts of his brain.

—*Is this what it means to feel the magical energy?*

And it wasn't only the magic energy; it felt as if he could see her breathing, her pulse, and even where she sweat using the palm of his hand. If you could train enough to get this kind of information by merely looking at someone instead of touching them, it was probable that you would catch on to Rem's secret, as well as the fact that Diablo was no ordinary Sorcerer.

He moved from her chest, and started to rub her exposed belly button.

Shera's back arched as she cried out.

"Hng!?"

"Hm!? Did that hurt…? No, it doesn't seem that way… What… is this? I can feel some kind of strange surge coming from her…"

Medios prompted him to continue.

"If something awful looks like it's going to happen, I'll make sure to stop it, so just keep on going"

"I see… I leave that to you, then."

He rubbed his middle finger against her belly button.

Shera's voice rang out once again.

"Nghhh! Mnnnnnn!"

"Does that tingle? Keep enduring it… The magic is concentrating just below here."

He touched the lower part of her stomach.

"Ah!? Aaaah! There… you can't! Not my stomach!!"

"This is where the magic is!"

He was slowly getting a grasp on the shape of the magic energy twisting and swirling inside of Shera.

Medios spoke up:

"Now, try and intervene with the magic energy. Just put it in slowly, deliberately, carefully… Like you're pouring honey into a bottle."

"Hm."

Diablo started to pour magic energy into Shera.

Slowly.

"Mnn!? Ah… Dia… blo… Fwah, mhm… For some reason… right below my stomach… It's starting to feel hot…!"

Medios happily nodded.

"Oh my, just what I would expect from someone Celestine holds in such high regard. In such a short period of time, you've broken through the outer layer and started to reach the core..."

"Is this enough?"

"It's not going to be enough if you keep going that slow. It seems like Shera's completely open right now, so how about just *spurting* it all in there?"

"Is that all right!?"

"Infusing someone with magic is the same thing as them drinking an MP potion. Once you can do that, then I can teach you how to use enslavement magic."

"All right... Here I go, Shera."

Her cheeks red and her breath ragged, tears formed in the corners of her eyes.

She gave a small nod.

"Y-Yeah, it's all right... You can... go ahead..."

He gathered magic energy into his hand, and just like when he would accumulate magic energy into Tenma's Staff, he poured it into Shera.

"Woooooahhhh!"

It was a sensation like he had broken through some kind of soft wall. It had been resisting him this whole time, but now, it was sucking him in.

Diablo released his magic energy inside of Shera. Her body twitched and convulsed.

"Ahh! Nhaa! Hyaaaaaaaaaaa!!"

A torrent of bright white light burst forth, filling his vision.

"...And so, when you see that, you can interfere with it just a little. Then you just have to tie it all together, like you're tying a shoelace." Using a piece of string, Medios manipulated her fingers to create some kind of shape. "You use your magic energy to tie everything nice and tight. Got it?"

She sat in her chair, legs crossed.

Arms folded, Diablo sat opposite of her. He was still feeling sluggish after having released his magic energy.

"That would still be hard for me unless I concentrated more... But I did feel like I could see it at points. If I could physically touch it, then everything would be perfect."

"Hehehe... It took me twelve years to learn that part, you know?"

"I am a Demon Lord. Do not compare me to the likes of the other races."

—*I've sunk countless hours into this stuff, after all... Well, in the game, at least.*

Perhaps it was because of his constant magic use in this world, but he had been able to learn a portion of this technique shockingly fast.

Medios shrugged her shoulders.

"But it just doesn't seem like it's going to work."

"I do not think that it is impossible. Judging by the duration of my concentration and precision with this technique, however, it doesn't seem like I stand much of a chance at the moment."

"I wonder if Shera's genius could have unconsciously prevented your success."

"It's possible."

"That may well be the reason it materialized so slovenly."

Diablo nodded in response.

He had seen the magic energy from Shera, as well as in the enslavement collar around her neck.

"It was like… being in a room with no end, with countless balls of yarn tangled over each other on the floor… And even though I would have to untangle them all one-by-one, the room was filled with smoke and my vision was limited, and I can only be in there as long as I can hold my breath…" Diablo said with a sigh.

"Bingo. How about just giving up now?"

"Ngh…"

He had no intention of doing so, but one thing was certain: he had a crushingly difficult task ahead of him.

Right next to them, sleeping peacefully with a blanket covering her, laid Shera. The enslavement collar still remained fastened around her neck.

Rem and Alicia exited the tent together. The guard outside greeted them:

"Please feel free to rest here," he said, guiding them towards a bench. "Sometimes, we have patrons who become ill, so this bench is always prepared. That goes especially for women."

Though the hustle and bustle of the marketplace could still be heard, the tent was a bit out of the way, so it wasn't that noisy around here.

Having accepted his offer, Rem was sitting on the bench, with Alicia next to her.

—*She seems like a nice person, but I don't know what to talk about.*

Rem usually tried not to get involved with people. Because of that, whenever she was with someone she wasn't familiar with, she wouldn't know what to do.

Then, just as she was feeling troubled—

Alicia started to talk with a gentle smile.

"What do you think is necessary for unraveling the mystery of how this 'enslavement magic' works?"

Rem thought a bit before answering.

"…I think it is most likely something similar to Summon magic."

"Like throwing crystals?"

"Ah... I meant the ritual magic needed to make contracts with Summons, not actually using it."

The magic used to first call a Summon and the magic to turn them into a crystal were both "Summon Magic." Fitting an explanation for this in as well, Rem continued to speak.

"...By finding a 'Place,' founding a 'Situation,' and finally, establishing a 'Role,' the spell activates... That is what I understand ritual magic to be. By casting the spell at Starfall Tower, the 'Place,' I created a 'Situation' brimming with magical energy. By establishing myself in the 'Role' of a Summoner, I called forth my Summon."

What actually appeared hadn't been a Summon, however.

"So I see." Alicia nodded. "As one would expect from Miss Rem, I take my hat off to your superior wisdom when it comes to magic."

"...It isn't like you are completely clueless about magic though, right?"

"I am fairly confident when it comes to martial arts, but with magic— I cannot even reach the footsteps of the experts. I haven't the faintest idea as to what this 'flow of magic energy' is that Lady Medios spoke of earlier."

"...I did not understand what she meant either... Though it was not like I couldn't make any guesses as to what it was."

Rem couldn't see the "flow of magical energy." It may have been because she lacked the ability to do so; but then again, she had never even done any training in the first place.

Medios had called it the result of "grueling and painstaking discipline..."

—But it did not seem like Shera had gone through any training, either.

Though she may seem like an airhead, Shera could be surprisingly sharp-witted at times. She wasn't in possession of a single Summon, but her talents seemingly lay elsewhere, like the ability to see the flow of magic energy.

Apparently, there were cases where those born into royalty came into the world with special blessings. These graces could be found in the blessing of the Harvest God, which would make it so the land you ruled had bountiful harvests; or the blessing of the Ocean God, which would calm the waves of the ocean and make it safe to travel by sea at any time. These were long-lasting effects that were impossible to achieve through magic, and would activate just by the person being alive.

Shera's abilities might be one of those blessings; her very existence itself was blessed.

—*The exact opposite of mine,* Rem thought.

Alicia had a look of concern on her face.

"Miss Rem, are you still feeling unwell?"

"…I'm fine," Rem answered, shaking her head. She was worried she had been curt with that answer, even though Alicia was only concerned for her sake.

Alicia didn't seem to be bothered in the slightest.

"Are you curious as to what that woman may be teaching Diablo and Miss Shera?"

"…There is that."

"I will wait here, so why don't you try going back in now?"

"…No… I'm not good with people like her…"

Rem placed a hand on her chest— The soul of the Demon Lord Krebskulm was sealed inside of her. Though she hadn't given Medios any information, the slave trader was on the verge of realizing this. Of course, even if Medios did realize there was another stream of magic inside Rem, it wasn't like she would make a direct connection of it belonging to a Demon Lord.

Alicia nodded.

"She does seem like the sort of person to see through everything, doesn't she… I was a little afraid of her as well."

"…Even though you are an Imperial Knight who would never tell a lie?"

"Hehe… Of course not. No one like that exists."

"What?"

"In fact, the more an Imperial Knight tries to be just and fair, the number of lies they tell becomes greater as well."

"…Is that true?"

"That's a secret, OK?"

Alicia playfully shrugged her shoulders.

—*So even an Imperial Knight like her has secrets.*

Alicia looked to be the perfect person: she was truthful, had a bright personality, and was very sociable. But even a woman like her still held secrets. Rem was somewhat happy to hear this.

She voiced her concerns; it felt like the kind of atmosphere she could do this in.

"…I was afraid of having my own secret revealed."

"I understand. Everyone carries some kind of secret, after all… When I feel like mine is going to be found out, I use a charm to keep it safe."

"A… charm?"

"It's a little childish, so I'm a bit embarrassed to say it."

Alicia stuck out her tongue. It was surprising for someone as mature as her to make this kind of gesture.

"…And what would that charm be?" Rem asked.

"Are you interested? Then… could you please close your eyes and give me your hand?"

"…Like this?"

Just as she was told, Rem closed her eyes and stuck out her hand. There was a slight tickling sensation from within the palm of her hand.

Alicia's finger traced a circle on Rem's palm, as well as various other lines. Suddenly, Rem's hand became warm: she felt magic energy.

—*She used magic!?*

Surprised, Rem's eyes flew open. Even Alicia had a startled look on her face.

"Huh?"

Neither one of them could speak right away.

Rem was the one to break the silence.

"…Alicia… What was that just now…?"

With a jolt, Alicia deeply bowed her head.

"U-Um, well… In my hometown, we have a tradition where one would draw a circle on their hand, then chant the magic words: 'Now it's closed.' That would help protect your secret…"

"…Is that right? I sensed some kind of magic."

"I-Is that so? I, too, was surprised that it suddenly sparked like that. Now that I'm thinking about it, this is the first time I have done this to a Sorcerer… Something may have happened due to the presence of your magic energy. I was careless— I apologize for surprising you like that."

Was it because magic was there in Rem's hand? Or could it have been because of the Demon Lord sealed inside her? No matter the case, if Alicia had realized the soul of the Demon Lord Krebskulm was sealed inside of Rem, she would have jumped far away by now.

Alicia hadn't drawn the sword at her waist; based on her current attitude, she wasn't lying. It seemed she still didn't know Rem's secret.

As Alicia humbly bowed her head, Rem spoke up.

"…It's all right. Please, do not worry yourself about it."

"Can you bring yourself to forgive me?"

"…It really is not that big of a deal, honest. I was just taken aback, that's all."

"Thank goodness! And thank you very much."

"…I feel a lot better after having talked with you."

Rem wasn't lying here. When Celes and Diablo found out about her secret, she had been absolutely terrified. But after they accepted her despite that, a great wave of relief had washed over her. It felt much different now when she only talked about it a little, even if she hadn't revealed her secret.

She could never be open about everything with an Imperial Knight like Alicia, though.

A gentle smile came across Alicia's face.

"I don't quite understand myself… But if I was able to be of use to you in some way, then I am happy. I would never want to ignore anyone like yourself, Miss Rem, who is dealing with something they cannot openly share with others."

That evening—

Diablo and the others returned to the large room they were renting out at the "Peace of Mind Inn - Twilight." He was pretty drained, feeling like the kind of exhaustion he retained after using his MP. It wasn't as bad as if he had used it all, but it still might have been a bit careless of him when they may be fighting against the Elves at almost any second.

Though you could tell the wall broken by the attackers had gone through repairs, the hole had been closed up tight. It was a shock something like that was fixed in only a single day. It might have been some kind of Earth-elemental magic; that, or the construction techniques of this world were just that good.

Diablo placed his war scythe near the bed. This was something he decided to keep out of his pouch, just in case of any more attackers.

He sat himself down on the bed. Rem sat next to him.

"…I feel particularly exhausted today, for some reason."

"Hm."

She had been stressed out and nervous since this morning, so it was no wonder she would feel that way.

Taking a quick glance, Diablo could see Alicia standing in the doorway. She looked like some kind of bodyguard.

Then there was Shera, who was standing stock-still.

"……"

"What's the matter, Miss Shera? Are you not feeling well?"

Just a little while ago, Diablo had poured his magic energy into Shera, as well as saw the magic energy that constructed her enslavement collar.

—I wonder if all that is starting to affect her now, Diablo worried.

Shera shook her head.

"No, I'm all right. Actually, I'm raring to go! But, it's just… When I think how much trouble everyone here has been through because of me… I'm so sorry…"

Rem immediately denied the sentiment.

"…You truly are a fool, aren't you. The cause of this strife is due to the Kingdom of Greenwood's arrogant demands, not because of you, Shera."

"Are you really sure…?"

"…While it may be true that the princess has run away from home, having the country she ran away from insinuate a declaration of war demonstrates a complete and utter lack of common sense. I cannot fathom Greenwood as that of a decent country after what they have done."

Alicia nodded in agreement.

"In my personal assessment, I must declare that I find the Kingdom of Greenwood's conduct to be strikingly disrespectful. They should understand that this situation causes Miss Shera to suffer."

Diablo felt the same. But if only he could properly express himself on delicate issues like this, then he wouldn't have so much trouble communicating with others.

He remained silent.

—You know, the more people there are, the less of a presence I feel I have here…

He shook the negative thought from his head. There was one thing that Diablo could do for Shera—

—I will avoid this war.

They were getting help from all kinds of people to do just that.

"Alicia, where will you be sleeping tonight?" Rem asked.

Rem, Shera, and Diablo were all staying in this room together. The room was big, but the bed was more than a bit cramped with three people in it. Four people would be just plain impossible. Depending on where he put his hands… "accidents" could also occur.

"I will be using the room next door, so there is no need to worry about me."

Rem had a disappointed expression on her face.

"…I see."

—They seem to be getting along better after Shera and I left them alone at the slave emporium. Rem doesn't seem to have a lot of friends, so that's a good thing.

Alicia placed a hand on the doorknob.

"I was just thinking everyone would need some time in private. My role is to act as His Majesty's eyes, and if necessary, as someone who conveys the thoughts of the Kingdom of Lyferia. I have no intention of observing what happens in your personal lives."

Diablo felt a bit relieved on the inside. If there ended up being three girls in the bed, it would probably be time for him to start sleeping on the floor.

On the surface, he calmly nodded.

"Do as you wish."

"Thank you very much. Then, if you will excuse—"

As she spoke, the haunting melody of a flute overlapped with her words.

†

The sound of a high-pitched whistle, like the sound a pipe would make, could be heard.

Though it gave the impression the player was musically skilled, the noise unpleasantly coiled and snaked its way through Diablo's ears.

The sound was getting louder, and closer.

It came right next to them. Even Diablo could clearly tell it was coming from the other side of the door.

It was right in front of their room.

Alicia, who was closest to the door, exchanged glances with Diablo as if she were asking, "What should we do?"

Diablo stood up, war scythe in hand.

"Open it."

Alicia opened the door.

There, an Elven youth was playing a fife. He had a handsome face, and was about the same height as Diablo. He was much more slender, though, giving him a gangly appearance. His hair looked as if it was made out of molten gold, and his feminine features presented an air of beauty. The corners of his eyes hung downwards, giving him an almost gleeful countenance.

But the vulgar smile he wore on his face put all his "good looks" to waste.

—*Maybe it's because he's an Elf, too, but doesn't he look kind of similar to her?*

Diablo looked at Shera; an expression of shock on her face, she unsteadily backed away.

"Wh-Why... Why are you here!?"

The Elf took the fife from his lips and put it into the sash around his waist.

"Heh heh… Your head is as empty as ever, I see… Why, you ask? I came to get you, of course."

"And that's why I'm asking! Why did you come all the way here by yourself, big brother!?"

—Big brother!? This guy is Shera's brother!? Then that means—

The Elven boy gave an elegant bow.

"Greetings and salutations. I am Keera L. Greenwood: Shera's brother, and royal prince of the sovereign Kingdom of Greenwood. Remember this well, you ignorant peasants."

The expression on his face was stained with scorn and contempt.

"How did you find out I was here!?" Shera shouted.

"Hah! Did you actually think you were hiding yourself? Come now, just try thinking about it— I heard it from the Adventurers. The amount I put out for your bounty was quite sum, after all. Everyone has at the very least investigated your whereabouts. All I had to do was show a little cash to persuade them with the information."

He said it as if it were nothing.

—Is this guy really the prince?

Just by looking at Shera's reaction, it didn't seem like there was any room for doubt… But having the prince of a nation come by himself, into the country he declared war on no less, was definitely strange.

—Would he actually take a risk like this? Or is it possible he's an imposter that even Shera couldn't tell apart from the real deal?

Keera looked at Diablo, a sneer on his face.

"Hm-hmm? So, you're the one who's turned her into a slave, are you? I bet she was easy to fool, wasn't she. Her head is as empty as the sky is blue, after all."

"I have not made her my slave." Diablo shook his head.

"Hmm? Is that right? But, you know… Unless she was a slave, there isn't any way she would be with the likes of some Demon with horns growing out of his head. It's repulsive."

The prince spat onto the floor.

—*What the hell does he think he's doing in a room that* we're *renting!?*

He wanted to let his anger take over, but held fast and resisted. He still didn't have enough information.

If this truly was the Prince of Greenwood, then it was Diablo's job to make Keera think that fighting against him was a bad idea. If he could do that, he could avoid the war.

Though Diablo was taken aback by his actions, in the end he was just a stupid prince.

—*To think he would actually come by himself into enemy territory! I'm gonna threaten him so bad he'll piss himself.*

"Heh heh heh… Very interesting, you Elf brat. I am the Demon Lord Diablo! I will turn you to cinders where you stand!"

"Hmm? Well if that's what you want, then that's fine by me," Keera said, repugnantly. "But if I don't return by a certain time… then a great number of Humans will die."

Rem leaned forward.

"What did you do!?"

"How about you try actually thinking about how I made it this far. Is everything above your neck just empty space? Even though this is a Human town, Elves are allowed in, too."

It was true there were tons of Demis in this town… And that included Elves.

"Of course that would happen, Elves and Humans are friends!" Shera answered back. "That's why you—"

"This town is soft, soft, soft! It's way too soft! Greenwood has basically declared war, and just when I expected that they would start restraining all the Elves, they let me through the gate with only a light baggage inspection! And in a town where I could get my hands on all sorts of weaponry!"

"Ngh..."

"Listen up, Demon. I'll only say this once, so carve it into that empty skull of yours! Just *try* putting so much as a scratch on me. If you do, the Elves spread throughout this town will start indiscriminately attacking every Human in Faltra!"

The rage Diablo felt inside of him was almost enough to boil his insides. These weren't the words of a representative of an entire nation—

They were the words of a criminal.

He had finally realized why Galford was so wary of the Elves, even after calling them a small faction. There was just no way to fight with all the Elves hiding in town.

Keera thought his safety was all but guaranteed thanks to his underhanded tactics. That's why he had the audacity to come by himself.

—*What should I do?*

If Diablo didn't strike back here, then they would be completely on Keera's terms; they wouldn't even be able to negotiate. Not only would he snatch Shera away, he might make even more lofty demands.

—*If I give in to his threats, I lose!*

Diablo took up his war scythe.

"You're going to kill the Humans of this town? Hmph... What about it?"

163

"What was that!?"

Keera's eyes flew open.

Rem and Shera gave voice to their shock, while Alicia seemed disturbed by his announcement.

Diablo had completely committed himself to his Demon Lord act.

"I am the Demon Lord Diablo… Did you think that the lives of the masses would stay my hand?"

"Are you being serious!?"

Keera started to back away.

War scythe at the ready, Diablo took a step forward.

"You have made a grave mistake… You may have thought you could use the lives of mere Humans to give yourself an advantage over me, but that is not so."

"A-Are you planning on going to war with the Elves!?"

"Just what are you saying? It's already started, hasn't it. Do you not call sending soldiers to an enemy country with the intent to kill a war?"

"Not yet! It hasn't started yet! If I can get back to the specified location by 8 PM, then that acts as a signal for all the Elves not to attack!"

"So I see… It looks like you narrowly avoided death. If you started killing townspeople blindly, I would have headed to the Kingdom of Greenwood to kill Elves in the same manner. This town is my territory. I would have to give a fitting punishment to those who would commit barbarous acts of violence here."

"Ha… Haha… We have the greatest elite squadrons of Elves gathered at the Kingdom of Greenwood, and countless treasures at our disposal. As if a single Demon like you could…"

Rem sighed.

"…I'm shocked. You haven't even looked into the person you're trying to negotiate with."

"What did you say, you Pantherian witch!?"

"…Just the other day, Diablo took out an entire army of one hundred Fallen at the Bridge of Ulug. Are you telling us you have some kind of plan that could protect your country from a Sorcerer like him?"

"At least make up a more believable story if you're trying to bluff," Keera snorted. "As if I'd believe that overblown farce."

"It's true, big brother. I saw it with my own two eyes. He made everything disappear in a flash of white light!"

Alicia nodded as well.

"It is precisely because he is such a capable person that Sir Galford has allowed Princess Shera to remain at this inn, rather than having her stay at his mansion. He recognizes Diablo's true power."

"…Tch."

Keera clicked his tongue, then shrugged his shoulders with a sigh.

"All right, all right, I got it. Then how about we settle this all peaceful-like, hm? I'm actually not planning on starting a war. I mean, that's just stupid— Why should I have to go to war when I'm asking for something that's already mine to simply be returned to me? That would be such a pain in the ass. Father doesn't want to go through with it either— That's why I came here to confirm something, but I got all heated up instead… How embarrassing."

"Oh hoh? And what would that be?" Diablo asked back. "Speak."

An irritable expression crossed Keera's face. He had probably never been talked down to like this before.

"…Damn Demon, acting like he owns the place… I came to confirm Shera's intentions."

"That seems surprisingly reasonable of you."

"The reason Father doesn't want to go through with this is because he thinks Shera left home of her own accord. Geez, how could you get any stupider. You left home because you were confused, and now you can't come back because you got turned into a slave. That's all there is to it, right? Shera is my property, after all. She should be returned to her *rightful* owner."

"I now understand how you think."

"That so? Then let's just check how she really feels. Of course she's going to want to come back, so I'll be taking her home."

Diablo had gone past feeling angry; he was purely stunned now.

—*With a brother like this, I can see why Shera left home.*

I just want to punch him in his stupid face...

But right now, I need to negotiate.

The fact that the townspeople were still in danger remained unchanged.

"Hmph... You seem fairly confident; but what will you do if Shera says she does not want to return?"

Keera spread his arms wide.

"Then I'll give up! Did you not understand anything I just said!? You really *are* all idiots here! Don't ask me, that's just embarrassing."

—*This is weird... Does he actually think Shera is going to say she wants to go back?*

Of course she wouldn't say it.

She left because she wanted to be free. Not only that, but she wasn't alone anymore; she had called Rem, and even Diablo her "comrades."

—*There's no way she would say she wants to go back.*

Or it might have been that this journey changed Shera. In the past, she might not have been able to oppose her brother if he had made demands like this.

Wouldn't that explain why she's been seeking power?

—*Shera is different now.*

"Very well, then listen carefully as you hear it with your own ears: how your little sister truly feels!" Diablo declared confidently.

Shera nodded.

"Keera! I'm—"

"Whoa, now!" Keera cut her off. "Just hold on there for a second!"

Shera had a look of uncertainty on her face.

"W-What?"

"The collar on your neck, that's what! We're on the brink of war here, you know. I've got an army acting on my orders right now. This is a big deal, something that's going to affect the relationship between our countries from here on! Don't you think it should be obvious to hear Shera's answer under fair circumstances?"

—*And what's "fair" about any of the stuff you've been doing, Princey. It's not only unfair, it's wrong.*

"The collar has nothing to do with it!" Shera shot back.

"Your head is as empty as ever, I see. You have an 'Enslavement Collar' on, and the owner of that collar is—shocker—*right over there.* Anyone would think that every answer you gave was being forced in a situation like this."

"Diablo doesn't give me orders, unlike you and Father!"

"Shut your damn mouth, Shera. You want me to hit you!?"

She flinched, obviously terrified.

Without thinking, Diablo was on the verge of physically attacking Keera. He grabbed and held down his right arm with his left hand. If Rem hadn't been holding on to the fringe of his cape, he might have lunged at the prince.

"…And what would you consider to be fair circumstances? You're not thinking to say that you want to bring her back to the Kingdom of Greenwood and ask her there, are you?" Rem asked.

167

Keera shrugged his shoulders, palms raised.

"Of course I wouldn't, geez. At the very least, being in a place with other people around is a no-go."

Alicia raised her hand.

"I will prepare another room. As an Imperial Knight, I would like to ascertain the details of this meeting in person, so may I have your permission to be present as well?"

"Are you stupid? Imperial Knights are basically the swords of the Lyferian King. No matter how you think of it, having a Human stay next to the princess of Greenwood gives you an advantage. There's not an ounce of fairness to that!"

"But leaving the two of you alone would be…"

"Hey, now. I came into *your* territory all on my lonesome. And why do you think I did that? To solve this all peacefully, of course! Once I hear how Shera truly feels, then no matter what she says, the war will be avoided. That's why I've gone through all this trouble."

"Ngh…" Alicia grimaced.

He was certainly being aggressive with his insistence, but it was true there was a chance the war could be avoided….

Only as long as he kept his promise that he would leave after Shera turned him down, that is.

Keera gave a deep sigh.

"Oh, for the love of— All right, fine. I'll compromise, just for you… Give me five minutes. That should be fine, right?"

"You… What exactly is your aim here?"

"I came prepared with all sorts of things to convince Shera, but if I can just try out one thing, then that should be enough. Once she hears me play my flute, then she'll definitely get homesick and say she wants to go back."

The reason Shera had fled her hometown wasn't for something that simple enough where her mind would change over a little flute concert.

Diablo was curious as to whether or not there was a reason for this.

"Are you trying to say the repulsive sound of that flute is your secret weapon?"

Even if he was trying to be moderate about it, "repulsive" was the only word fitting enough for the fife. If that was able to change Shera's mind, he would start doubting her sensibility.

"Ha! So you don't even understand the sound of this instrument. Demons really are a race of uncivilized savages, aren't they," Keera spat out.

—*Is it really because I'm a Demon that I can't understand it?*

Looking around the room…

Rem, Alicia, and even Shera tilted their heads, looking confused.

—*The sound that flute thing makes isn't good after all. Keera is just talking it up by himself.*

There was no "flute" item in Cross Reverie that could affect your opponent. Diablo had a grasp on all the equipment implemented in the game, but no matter how much he dredged through his memories, there wasn't anything he could remember that looked similar to Keera's flute.

—*If that's true, then his chances of winning are so low it's practically disgusting. If this is the only condition he's putting up, I guess I'll give it to him.*

"What do you want to do?"

Not just Diablo— Rem and Alicia were looking at Shera.

He could tell that she was afraid. This was probably terrifying for her…

But still, she nodded.

"I'll do my best! Even if it's just the two of us, I'm going to tell my brother how I feel!"

"Are you sure?"

"Yeah… I'm scared of being alone with him, but if I can say it… If I can just say it, then there won't be any war. I promised I would do my best to stop it!"

Diablo nodded.

"…If he lays even a finger on you, scream. I will destroy him in an instant."

"Yeah. I'll be counting on you, Diablo. But it'll be all right… Despite how he is, we're family."

Rem and Alicia offered words of encouragement as well.

Keera waved his hands to clear them out afterwards.

"All right, that's settled then! Go on now, out go the pests. Geez, it was starting to reek of the uncivilized in here."

"I will say this now, Keera: the only things allowed are talking and your little musical performance. If you raise so much as one finger against her, I will reduce you to ash."

"Yeah, yeah, I'll keep my promise. I'll even swear on my pride as an Elf. Of course, if Shera says she wants to go back, you take off that enslavement collar, got it?"

Diablo shook his head.

"Impossible. I cannot remove it."

"Are you screwing with me?"

"Keera, it's true. We just looked into it again today, and not even slave traders or the Mage's Association could get it off…" Shera said painfully.

"Tch… What a bunch of useless idiots, incapable of undoing their own magic… But whatever. I'm sure we'll be able to do something using one of our treasures back home. At least make sure to remove any commands you have on her, then!"

"I have not given her any commands. She is not a slave."

"What? You were actually *serious?* I can't even begin to fathom how stupid you are… Aha, I get it. Shera's head is pretty much full of air, so you don't even need to use magic to give her orders. Well, congratulations one and all, your idiocy has surpassed my wildest expectations."

Diablo opened his mouth, lacing every word with the anger he appreciated today:

"And you. Give your word that if Shera says she will not return, you will pull out your troops and never interfere again."

A sneer on his face, Keera nodded.

"Fine by me. If she says no, I'll withdraw my troops tomorrow and we'll head home."

"It'll be over in a flash!" Shera said, smiling.

Diablo was uneasy, but he decided to put his faith in Shera. He was doubtful that he could trust the verbal promise Keera made…

But unfortunately, if he resorted to force, then he wouldn't be able to protect the people of this town.

For these negotiations—

Diablo had to line up cards Keera wouldn't like; not let him call their bluff; and make him fold. That's all there was to do.

Diablo left the room, taking Rem and Alicia with him. Leaving the two siblings behind, he shut the door.

†

The dining hall of the inn—

A lively place bustling with Demis who came to get dinner.

Diablo, Rem, and Alicia were sitting down, not ordering anything.

They had promised him five minutes.

Five, and only five minutes.

The sound of a flute could be heard.

—*So he is forcing her to listen to him play... It's such a creepy song; is he really that confident about it?*

It had looked like Shera reacted negatively to it as well.

Diablo found the music pouring into his ears to be extremely unpleasant.

And then, while still having not one single clue as to how this could sound good to anyone, it stopped.

"Alicia, how much time left?"

"Ten more seconds," she said, squinting at a pocket watch emblazoned with the Imperial Knights insignia.

It was an exceptionally high-class item in this world. Everything about it was handmade from scratch, down to every last minute detail and cog. It was worth its own weight in gold.

They heard the sound of feet descending the stairs—

Keera appeared. As usual, he had a smug smile plastered across his face.

Shera was nowhere to be seen.

Diablo confronted Keera.

"What happened with Shera?"

"You're asking *me* what happened? If she's not here, she must be in the room, duh. You don't have to think too hard to figure that one out, do you?"

"...If you are not together, I can only assume she must have said she isn't going back?" Rem asked.

"Ask her yourself. If I told you she said as such, would you believe me? Are you stupid?"

"...That is true... I lost my composure there."

—*So that was the only thing she was really worried about.*

Passing by Keera, Rem climbed up the stairs, Alicia following behind her.

Diablo glared at Keera.

"You will keep your promise, then."

"You're like a broken record, you know that? But, Demon—Diablo, was it? There's something I want to say to you."

"What?"

"The most important thing is for us to respect Shera's intentions, yes? I just want to make sure you know that. If Shera has a change of heart, no matter how much you may not like it, no complaining or moaning about it, got it? If she says she wants to go back home, you could force her to stay using that enslavement collar, so let's make that off-limits."

"That should be obvious."

"All right, you said it yourself. Then I guess I'll take my leave. If I get lost and don't make it back by eight, then this town would be in trouble, wouldn't it?"

"If you try *anything*, I'll make you regret it as you burn alive."

"Haha, I won't, I won't. Oh, that's right... Shera still seems to be wondering what to do, but she should realize how she really feels soon enough. When that happens, make sure you get all her stuff together, will you?"

"You promised you would take your forces and leave. Are you planning on going back on your word?"

Keera shrugged his shoulders.

"Unlike you, I was actually raised properly. I'll keep my promise; I'll pull out my troops tomorrow... Though when that happens, Shera will probably be with me, too."

—*Shera must have said she wasn't going back... But then why is he acting like this?*

With a triumphant sneer on his face, Keera left the inn.

†

Diablo returned to their room.

Shera was there, as they had hoped, sitting on the bed with Rem. Alicia remained standing in the doorway.

—*Is she trying to be a bodyguard or something?*

Even though she seemed exhausted, Shera was smiling.

"Welcome back, Diablo."

"Hm."

Rem sighed.

"...I didn't believe he would actually try to give a performance with that appalling flute."

"Right? I wonder what was up with that song he played? It made my head feel all itchy, I hated it!"

"...Did you talk with him at all?"

"Just a little... We talked about the past. He's not here anymore, but we talked about our older brother... and what's going to happen from now on. He told me that if I don't go back now, I'll never be able to again."

"...That's..."

Rem grimaced.

—*So he made her choose between going back or throwing away her hometown.*

She must still have friends and family there, other than her brother and father. It had to have been a tough decision to leave them behind...

Despite this, another smile came over Shera's face.

"It's fine! I decided I wasn't going back ever since I left home!"

"...Are you sure you're all right with that?"

"Yeah, I am. I feel so much better when I think about how I won't have to worry about being chased anymore, and how I won't cause trouble just by being here."

Her voice sounded cheerful... But something about it felt different than usual.

—*She might be depressed after all. That, or she's still worrying about something.*

"Thinking back to it," Alicia spoke up, "our meal earlier was too late to be lunch, and too early to be dinner... Are you hungry at all?"

Shera stepped down, off the bed.

"Now that you mention it, I'm starving!"

Rem smiled.

"...I feel a bit hungry as well."

"Ahaha, let's go eat something! I want something nice and crunchy, with nuts!"

"...It has to be meat."

"Thank you, Rem. And thanks to you, too, Diablo and Alicia! For some reason, I'm really hungry all of a sudden. I'm gonna eat even more than usual today!"

"...Just don't eat so much you get fat."

"Hm? No matter how much I eat, I don't seem to get fat, though."

"...Stupid high-fatty Shera."

"That's mean!!"

Rem left the room, with Shera chasing after her.

Alicia gave a wry smile.

"Hehe... It's nice having it be so lively, isn't it."

"I don't like having things this noisy," Diablo replied, just like a true Demon Lord would—

But he couldn't hold back his smile as he said it.

It finally felt like things had gone back to normal around here.

†

Late that night—

Diablo felt like it was only his consciousness that was awake; but not like he was actually up. Even though his body was exhausted, he was still awake— That was the kind of feeling he was getting.

The Faltra region had a warm climate, so he wasn't cold.

He peered out of half-opened eyes. The room was almost completely pitch-black.

—*What time is it right now?*

They didn't have a clock; if there was sunlight streaming through the small window of their room, then that meant it was time to get up. But right now, the room was still dark.

Suddenly, he noticed Shera, standing near the window. She looked to be lost in thought, staring up at the sky. The moonlight made her golden hair sparkle.

It was an almost holy image. He felt like he now knew why Elves were considered the race closest to Celestials.

—*I wonder what she could be thinking about?*

Diablo couldn't find the words to call out to her, and just stared.

He could hear Rem's voice.

"…Having trouble sleeping?"

Rem swung her legs over the side of the bed, sitting on the edge.

Shera was slightly surprised.

"You can't sleep either, Rem?"

"…I do not trust Prince Keera at all. I stayed awake in preparation for a surprise attack."

"Ahaha… No one seems to trust my brother. Well, I can certainly see why though…"

They both thought Diablo was asleep, so they kept their voices down.

"…What were you doing?" Rem asked again.

"Mm… Thinking about lots of things, I guess? I was remembering a bunch of stuff, like my memories back home, and about all that's happened on my travels. Things like that."

"…So you were feeling sentimental?"

"Yeah, that! That's what I wanted to say!"

"…Don't talk so loud. You're going to wake Diablo up."

"Oh, sorry."

Shera covered her mouth with both hands.

—*I'm already awake, though.*

He didn't know how to call out to the girls. It would be hard to jump into the conversation now, so he stayed quiet; but that turned into him eavesdropping on them. He didn't want to be rude, so he was planning on going back to sleep… But now that he was all nervous because of this weird situation, he didn't feel sleepy at all, even though he was indeed tired.

The two of them continued their conversation.

"…What are you going to do from now on, Shera?"

"From now on?"

"You shouldn't be chased after by the Elves anymore, so I see no reason for you to continue your work as an Adventurer. Do you not have some kind of dream or goal in mind?"

"Hmm… Do I really not have a reason to keep being an Adventurer?"

"…If you're doing it simply because you want to then I won't make you stop, but being an Adventurer is dangerous work. If the only reason you wanted to become stronger was because you did not want to be forcibly taken back home, then I would think there isn't any reason for you to continue."

"Oh, I see your point."

"...If you are going to keep being an Adventurer, then in that case, I will look after you as your senior."

"Really!?"

"...But this isn't something that you can do forever, so it would be a good idea to think of another way to make a living once you retire from being an Adventurer. You do have a future after all, Shera."

"Haha, you have a future as well though, don't you Rem?"

"...That... That is true."

Rem had become an Adventurer because she wanted to expel Krebskulm's soul from her body and destroy it.

It was an almost insurmountable task. Because of that, she probably hadn't been thinking about her own future.

—But I'll defeat the Demon Lord Krebskulm!

That was the promise he made.

Not privy to this information, Shera cocked her head to the side.

"You sure are weird, Rem! Then, um, you're asking about what I want to try doing, right?"

"...I feel like you are misunderstanding something here... But yes, let's go with that."

"Then I want to try running a café!"

"...A café?"

Rem's voice was a little incredulous.

Shera gave a vigorous nod.

"Aren't cafés amazing? You can drink coffee, get a bite to eat, and everyone has so much fun there!"

"…That is a very lax image you have."

"That's because I haven't been to one yet! You won't find any of them unless you go the Royal Capital, right?"

"…There are also some in Faltra. They were built recently."

"What! There are!? Where!?"

"…You're being too loud… I have never been there myself, but they should be in the Central District. Places like the governor's mansion have them."

"Woo, let's go there next time! Actually, let's go tomorrow!"

"…You sure seem hasty. We don't even know where they are, specifically. I plan on telling Celes what happened at the slave emporium tomorrow, so I will ask her where the cafés are located after that."

"Yay!"

Shera gripped her fists, looking truly ecstatic.

Rem chuckled, a smile playing on her face.

"…I'm sure it won't be a cheap place, but it will be my treat tomorrow. We shall celebrate your decision to be free."

"Aha, thank you! That's another step closer to my dream!"

"…I see."

"And then, and then! Once I open the café, I would be the owner; Rem, you'd be a waitress; and Diablo would be the guy who cleans the cups!"

"…Why are Diablo and I getting mixed up in your dream?"

"It's fine! It'll be fun if all three of us are doing it!"

"…I have my own plans for the future."

"Then your kids can come work in my café! How about it? Doesn't it sound amazing?"

"…Why are you obsessing over me so much?"

"Because you're the first friend I made after leaving home!" Shera said matter-of-factly.

"...Your first... friend...?"

Rem's voice shook slightly.

"That's right! I can't go back home anymore... But if you and Diablo are here, then the café will be my new place I want to come back to."

"...Shera, are you sure won't regret this?"

"Yup. I'm sure, I'm sure! Believe me, I made my decision not to go back, and I'm sticking with it. Though I may just be a teensy bit sad... But as long as you and Diablo are here, I'll be fine! Okay?"

"...Okay. I will believe you."

"I really am glad that I met everyone. If you and Diablo weren't around for me... I'm sure I would've been dragged back home. You two aren't just my saviors; you're my friends. You're more like family than my actual family."

Shera scratched her cheek, embarrassed.

Rem cast her eyes downwards.

"...When you say it like that... Um... It's embarrassing, but... I will not deny that."

"Hehe!"

"...But I'm sorry to say that I cannot be a part of your plans for the future."

"O-Oh..,"

Shera's shoulders slumped.

Standing up, Rem walked over to Shera.

"...Please, listen very carefully."

"What?"

Diablo was shocked.

—*Is she planning on telling Shera her secret!?*

"...I have a certain problem I'm dealing with right now. As long as this problem remains unsolved, I don't have the luxury of thinking about the future. Not only that, but this issue is extremely difficult to handle... Almost despairingly so."

Rem said each word slowly and deliberately.

"I-Is there anything I can do?"

"...I do not know."

"Then we have Diablo for that!"

"...That is true, Diablo may be able to do something about it. If he lends me his power, I think there is a possibility. That's why..."

Rem faltered.

Shera tilted her neck.

"That's why...?"

"...That's why, if you will still accept me, even after my problem is solved... I might be all right working a café with you."

Her cheeks flushed red.

Shera jumped towards her, wrapping her arms around Rem and falling onto the bed with her.

"Reeeeem!!"

"Hyah!?"

The two of them dove on top of Diablo, landing on him with an audible thud.

—Heblegh—

If Diablo didn't have his level 150 body, he probably would have made a sound like a frog that was getting crushed.

"Wh-What are you thinking!? Are you *trying* to wake Diablo up!?" Rem protested.

"Ah, sorry...! But, I was just so happy!"

—I think there's something wrong with you if you didn't think I'd wake up from that.

Diablo managed to get by by pretending he was still asleep.

While still on top of him, they continued talking.

"…Happy?"

"I mean, I bet Diablo will solve your problem in a flash!"

"…You make it sound so easy."

"I have to do my fair share, too! Starting up a café is gonna take some money, so I'm gonna keep on being an Adventurer!"

"…Very well. I think you're more suited to use a bow, but if you still want to be a Summoner, then I will assist you in acquiring your first Summon."

"But Diablo is already my Summon!"

"……What?"

"If you don't hurry up and get a Summon as strong as my Diablo, you're going to end up losing to me, Rem!"

"…I just cannot fathom this. When exactly did Diablo become *your* Summon? Explain to me clearly and precisely the contractual link between you two, and prove to me when you and Diablo mutually agreed to and decided upon said arrangement."

"Um, well… Today… Everything got kinda fuzzy when I was with him, so I think that settles it."

"…Are you an optimist, or just that dumb?"

"I wonder?"

"…Just go to sleep. I have to be up early tomorrow as well."

With a yawn, Rem returned to her original position in the bed, lying down on Diablo's right side.

However, Shera was still clinging to her.

"Noooo way!"

"…You should be on the left. We already decided that your place was on Diablo's left side," Rem said, annoyed.

This was the first time Diablo had heard about this agreement.

But Shera still would not let go.

"No! I'm gonna sleep while cuddling you, Rem!"

"...You're being annoying."

"Well! If you're going to say that... then I'll do this!"

"Ah!? G-Grabbing someone's ears like this, ngh... What are you thinking!?"

"I've always wanted to try touching them!"

—*I totally know how you feel.*

Rem's body shuddered.

"Hahn!? N-No... even though... Diablo was the only one... to do this to me!"

"What!? He did? Like this? He was touching me today, too...."

"What!? Ah! Back at the slave emporium!?"

"Yup, that's right. And then, he went to my stomach, just like this..."

"Hng!? Why are you using *my* stomach to reenact it!?"

"And then, we take magic energy..."

"Magic energy!?"

"Then, hmm... Even though I can see it, I've never tried putting magic energy into anyone. How about... Maybe like this?"

"S-Stop! Stop this— Mm! Hnnnng!!"

"Yup, that's totally the voice you make when it feels good!"

"Ngh... Stupid Sheraaaaa! Nhaaaaa!?"

"Oh, so *this* is what it means to put magic energy into someone! Makes you feel all warm and tingly below your stomach, right? And now, the main event..."

Rem's body was trembling. She was touching Diablo's shoulder, so he could feel her shaking as well.

There was no way Diablo was going to be able to sleep now.

After screaming, Rem passed out as if she had fainted. And once Shera had fallen asleep from fatigue after releasing her MP—

Diablo lay awake in silent anguish, unable to sleep even after morning came.

†

The next morning—

After eating breakfast, Diablo and the others split up to do their own things. They were all taking care of their reports of what had happened:

Rem said she was going to the Adventurer's Guild to talk to Sylvie, and then make her report to Celes, while Alicia was heading to see the governor. It seemed they would both be back before noon.

Diablo would only end up coercing those he talked to, so he stayed behind at the inn. Shera was with him as well, the official reason being she was "probably tired."

They still hadn't confirmed whether or not Keera had actually made his retreat. It would be stupid of him to let Shera get kidnapped because he had left her by herself.

That said, he couldn't afford to spend his time lazing about the room. He had managed to avoid a war this time, but if he neglected being prepared now, it would just lead to unease later. As Diablo didn't have a stockpile of potions on hand, and since he was still using the Demon Lord's Ring, this was a problem just waiting to happen.

With a heavy thud, Diablo sat himself down on the floor. He had really wanted to do this at a desk, but there wasn't any other furniture in this room besides the bed.

Plunging his hand into his pouch, he tried imagining what he wanted to take out—

First up was a potion flask. Keeping an image of it in mind, his fingers hit something hard, which he grabbed and pulled out. A small metallic test tube, longer than the pouch itself, came sliding out.

—Putting things in and taking things out doesn't seem to be a problem, at least.

He had experimented with it multiple times, and had even used it to store Tenma's Staff, so he would be in trouble if something happened now.

He took out a few more items: "forest poppy leaves" and "fresh spring water", as well as the "Combiner set" he had first received when choosing his sub-class. It was a pestle and mortar, though it was his first time actually seeing one. The pestle was a rounded rod, and also ceramic. It had a cylindrical shape for the most part, while the tip was kept thick and round to crush ingredients.

—So I just grind it all up, and all should be good as gravy...

But will it really?

Does it become a potion if I just crush it like that? If it's that easy, is there even any point to picking the Combiner subclass?

Diablo pondered things over, staring at his tools and ingredients.

"Di~a~blo? Whatcha doing?"

Shera was crouching opposite of Diablo, peering at him curiously.

—How should I answer that?

If he was confident that he was going to succeed, he would just be honest and say he was going to combine things together to make potions—but failure was still a possibility here. At the very least, Diablo had no knowledge of medicine in Medieval times.

He decided to try and give himself some insurance, so that even if he did mess up, it would still be all right.

"I was thinking about trying to recreate the potions I had in my world."

"Oh, you're making potions?"

185

"Yes. However, these ingredients look similar to what I had in my world, but actually are not. This is an experiment to see what kind of results I can get from them."

—*That's a big fat lie.*

He was planning on using it as an excuse to say: "Yep, these ingredients are different from the ones in my world. If they're different, they won't work. Yep," in case he failed.

—*Putting that aside, how do I make this?*

He had the ingredients—

He had the tools—

He had the motivation—

He just didn't know how.

Shera got down on all fours, staring at his hands.

"Hey, aren't you going to make it?"

"…I'm concentrating right now."

"Wow, you look like you're gonna make something amazing! I promise I'll be quiet, so it's okay if I watch, right?"

"O-Of course."

He knew she meant no harm, but he felt like it was putting more pressure on him, and he was being driven into a corner, mentally.

He grabbed some of the forest poppy leaves.

—*Do I just put this in the mortar and mash it up? Or does it need some kind of extra step?*

I was hoping that if I just focused, the knowledge would come flowing to me…

But, unfortunately, nothing happened.

Shera was looking at him like a curious kid; but the one part of her that definitely wasn't childish was swaying slightly. As she leaned over across from him, it looked like he could almost see the tips of her chest.

—Is this for real!?

Who the hell cares about the potion anymore. I'd rather have some lotion right now, actually... I have no idea what I'm saying anymore. Super! Amazing! Boobs!!

"Ah!" Shera exclaimed loudly.

"Hm!? Ah, no, you see... I-I was just looking at one of the buttons on your clothes—"

"That's amazing! I can't believe you can make it that fast! That's my Diablo for you!"

"Hm?"

—What is she talking about?

Diablo looked at his hands. The forest poppy leaves he should have been holding had suddenly turned into a potion flask. Not only that, but it was stopped off with a cork; and judging by its weight, it was filled to the brim.

"Oh?"

"I've seen potion-makers before, but none of them were this fast!" Shera exclaimed excitedly.

"Wh-What part... was fast about it?"

"Mmm, everything!"

"Try saying some of the steps you saw me go through."

What he really wanted to say: "Please tell me, what the hell did I just do?"

"It was so fast that I don't really know myself," Shera said as she started to explain. Apparently, he had first removed parts of the poppy leaves, then put the remaining bits into the mortar and mashed them up with the pestle. Then, he added small amounts of the fresh spring water, doing so about ten times while starting to add the other parts of the leaves he had put aside earlier, little by little.

—In that short amount of time? In the time for her boobs to bounce three times?

There's no way I can do that again, even if she explains it to me…

I don't even know what parts of the leaves I removed, or even the right time to add them in…

It sounded like the work of a true craftsman.

—Basically, that means when I make a conscious effort to move my hands, they're the hands of someone who doesn't know anything about making potions…

But if I'm focused on something else, my hands move unconsciously; they become the hands of an experienced "Combiner".

So I just have to distract myself, then?

"Are you not going to make any more?" Shera tilted her head curiously.

"Oh, uh… I am, but… Ahem! Shera, watch carefully. If you are an Adventurer, then it would be for the best if you are able to make this, too. So watch only my hands! And closely!"

"Yeah! I'm watching!"

Eyes still sparkling, Shera stared at Diablo's hands. And as for him—

He stared at her chest.

White.

Round.

Her soft-looking chest would change shape slightly as she moved her body.

—This is truly a dangerous foe…

Have to make sure I don't start panting.

Just a little more, and I can see the tip…

The tip!!

With a short gasp, Diablo looked at his hands: there were nine potion flasks rolling around on the ground.

—Hell yeah, nice job Mr. Expert Combiner!

"That's amazing!" Shera cheered, clapping her hands.

To be honest, he had felt a hint of regret at the way he'd gone about it, but at least he learned he could create potions in this world.

"Well... I still need to test it out."

"Test what?"

"If this potion can actually be put to use or not. I had planned on this being something to recover one's health, but..."

"Want me to try drinking it?"

"No, there's no point in making you drink it if you aren't wounded. I'll try it out the next time someone gets hurt. With the ingredients I used, even if this ends up being a dud, it at least won't be able to poison you."

Even if it was a success, it wouldn't even heal one percent of Diablo's total HP. It wasn't exactly something he could rely on in battle. Once he could get his hands on some rarer ingredients and make an MP potion, that's when he would try using it on himself. There was no longer any pressing situation that might require potions, but it was still best to be prepared.

He had managed to avoid a war, and according to Shera, Keera should be pulling out his troops and returning home today.

—*If he keeps his promise, that is.*

Keera couldn't be trusted, which is why Diablo still couldn't afford to let his guard down now.

A flute's whistle—

Diablo had heard this repulsive melody before.

—*Keera's flute.*

Not only has he not retreated yet, but he actually came back into town... He didn't have any intention of keeping his promise after all.

Diablo swiftly packed up his potion-making materials, shoving them into his pouch. Grabbing his war scythe, he stood up and went to the window to survey what was going on outside:

There was an exceedingly fancy carriage parked outside the inn, out of place for this area of town—

But he couldn't see anyone who was holding a flute.

Then, all of a sudden, the music stopped.

—Did he leave?

Keera was still nowhere to be seen, so Diablo returned to where he had been in the room.

Shera was still crouched over, frozen in the same position as she was before. The sound of that flute may have reminded her of the painful choice she made yesterday.

Diablo checked to see how she was doing. Shera had a thousand-yard stare, as if she were not looking at anything in particular. Her lips were moving ever so slightly as she mumbled indistinctly under her breath.

Diablo became worried.

"Hey, Shera! What's wrong!? Get ahold of yourself!"

Shera looked at him.

"Oh, Diablo…. What's up?"

She was the same as always. It looked like she had been shaken up for a moment, but now she was back to normal.

"Are you all right?"

"What do you mean?"

"Well… If you're all right, then it's fine."

"Oh yeah, that's right… Um, you know what? I have something I need to tell you Diablo, is that okay?"

It was an abrupt request.

"What is it?"

"Well, I have to tell you…"

Her gaze wandered. Diablo couldn't even begin to guess what she was going to say, so all he could do was wait. She stared at Diablo with an ambiguous expression on her face, as if she were on the verge of either crying or laughing.

While fidgeting around, pressing her fingers together, she opened her mouth:

"I'm going back to the Kingdom of Greenwood."

—*What… did she just say?*

He couldn't comprehend what she had said. Had he misheard?

As Diablo remained silent, Shera continued to speak:

"U-Um, you see… I have to go back. The Kingdom of Greenwood is my home, after all. If I don't make a successor with my brother, then the royal line will die out. Keeping the royal family going is much more important than my own freedom."

"That can't… be."

"Oh, but this isn't like a sense of duty on my part or anything. When I thought about it more, it's kind of because of how much I respect my brother… and if I go back home, I don't have to keep doing dangerous work as an Adventurer. Throwing away a stable lifestyle for the sake of freedom is just stupid, right?"

"I… suppose you could think about it that way."

—*What…? What is going on!?*

Shera should have turned down Keera's proposal. Diablo had learned how much Shera wanted to stay in Faltra after her talk with Rem last night. So why did it turn out like this all of a sudden?

—*What is this sudden change of heart? Is it even possible to change your mind this fast?*

Had she been hiding how she really felt while talking with Rem? Is Shera even capable of doing something like that?

"Ah, gotta get my things together... But I guess I didn't really have much with me, anyways."

Shera began packing her things into a leather bag. As Diablo watched her, a flurry of thoughts ran through his mind.

—*Did I do something to hurt her feelings?*

He began to feel like he had. He was bad at picking up on how others felt, and he was fully aware that he was a good-for-nothing person. If he was actually good at connecting with other people, then he wouldn't have spent all his time playing games by himself. Had he ended up stepping on one of Shera's personal landmines because of this?

—*I don't know.*

He couldn't even begin to know what Shera was thinking.

—*I don't know...*

Is it because I did something wrong?

I just don't know...

Now finished with packing her things, Shera stood up.

"See you, Diablo."

Diablo's mind was in disarray.

"Well, um... I will at least see you off."

"Thanks."

All the while, Shera had kept that ambiguous expression on her face.

They had left the room. Still bewildered at the turn of events, Diablo followed after Shera as they descended the stairs, walking to the entrance of the inn.

"Are you not going to say goodbye to Rem?" Diablo asked.

"Never mind that, I have to hurry it up and return home with my big brother."

—*She won't even say her goodbyes to Rem!?*

And just when they were getting along so well together.

—*What is with this sudden change of heart? Or was it an act all along...? Would there even a point to that?*

Diablo couldn't believe it.

Without hesitation, and without even looking back, Shera left the inn. A carriage was waiting just outside, the same one Diablo had seen from the window. He started to hear the straining notes from that grotesque flute as the door to the carriage slowly opened.

—*It* was *him after all.*

Fife in hand, with a look of scorn and contempt plastered across his face— It was Keera.

"Hurry up and get in, Shera, before the stink of Demon gets on me... Or should I say, the smell of a loser!"

It was as if Keera had expected this to happen all along.

Shera climbed into the carriage.

"Heh heh..." Keera gave a throaty laugh. "You understand, don't you, Demon? The most important thing for us is to respect Shera's intentions, right? Make sure you keep your promise: no complaining if she says she wants to go back home."

Diablo couldn't say anything back as Keera's sneer washed over him.

The carriage door slammed shut: Shera didn't even look back outside. In fact, it didn't seem like she was looking anywhere. She resembled a statue the way she had stiffened up.

The carriage began to move—

And just like that, Shera disappeared from Diablo's side.

†

He stood there until the carriage was no longer visible. The people around him passed by, staring at him for a second before moving on.

—What… just happened?

I really don't know.

A whirlwind of thoughts swirled around in his head before disappearing, leaving almost as fast as they came. He stood there frozen like that for who knows how long.

Rem and Alicia called out to him; apparently, they had returned.

"…I never thought you would actually come out to greet us," Rem said, tilting her head. "Were you worried that we were taking too long to come back? Call Shera so we can have lunch together… You haven't eaten yet, have you?"

"After going through what she has, it would be nice if eating a bit earlier helped her regain some of her energy," Alicia said, a gentle smile on her lips.

"…Well, that is true."

A whirlpool of questions still going through his head, he gave a mechanical reply.

"Shera… went back to the Kingdom of Greenwood…"

Rem and Alicia's eyes widened:

"…!?"

"What…!?"

They seemed to have been at a loss for words, as they were unable to say anything. It must have been quite the shock for them.

The look on Alicia's face was particularly solemn.

"I do not mean to doubt your words, but is that the truth? I find it very hard to believe."

"Yes… It is… I have no idea what changed in her head either. I just watched her leave."

He looked in the direction the carriage had disappeared.

Rem drew closer to Diablo.

"Did you say something to Shera!? Something that, um… something that would make her leave!?"

"I didn't… All I did today was make some potions. But there must have been something she didn't like about me… It happens all the time…"

"Of course this doesn't happen all the time! W-We have to catch up with her!"

"We can't. She left by carriage. Keera was here waiting for her, just like they had planned it or something… Maybe she was planning to do this ever since they had that private talk with each other. Not that I'd know, though…"

These didn't sound like things Diablo would say— But he didn't have the energy to care.

Turning his back on the two of them, he headed towards the inn.

"…What are you going to do?" Rem asked.

"Sleep."

He went back inside the inn. He could hear Rem's voice coming from behind him—

Ignoring her, Diablo returned to the room.

†

Throwing himself on the bed, Diablo stared at the ceiling.

—*I feel like this always happens…*

He had misjudged her.

—I think I've actually gotten close to someone…
I think they might feel the same way about me—
But it's all just a mistake on my part.

They would let it be known they thought of him as worthless, hurting him as they pleased.

—It had only seemed like Shera was connecting with everyone else…

She had never seemed like the kind of person skillful enough to pull off a lie like that… But even that was just an act. From the very beginning, had she just been hanging around with us on a whim?

No, our bond with Shera was the real thing…

But that could just be another wrong assumption on my part…

A never-ending thought cycle.

He heard a knock on the door. The sound pulled Diablo out of the murky swamp of thoughts in his head—

He didn't respond.

The one knocking entered the room:

Rem.

"…No matter how you look at it, I find Shera's actions to be impossible for her."

She wasn't criticizing her; she was probably announcing the result of her thinking this over rationally.

Diablo stayed silent.

"…That dumb Elf isn't capable of putting on an act like this," Rem continued. "If she could, then she would have gotten straight to the point and tried to make things more profitable for herself. She's not that bright, and has a terrible memory… In the beginning, she had tried to hide the fact she was royalty, remember? But even so, she still went out of her to say the name 'Greenwood' when she introduced herself. That's how much a fool she is. She isn't capable of lying."

—*That's true...*

If Shera really wanted to hide the fact she was royalty, she could have just made up some fake name.

But Shera hadn't done that. Even though there weren't any advantages to *not* doing it.

"...It has to be some kind of magic," Rem declared. "There are spells that can manipulate someone's will, after all."

Diablo had thought of this possibility as well.

"But... It didn't look like she was being controlled at all. At the very least, there's no magic I know of that lets you force someone to say something that clearly."

"It didn't seem as awkward or as forced as before."

When they had first met, Diablo had given Rem and Shera an "order" without intending to: "Make peace by shaking hands... and with a smile!" And at that time, the two of them had exchanged handshakes, smiles on their faces.

But even then the two of them still complained while doing it, and the smiles on their faces clearly showed they weren't enjoying it. Even though they were forced to shake hands, it didn't change how they felt about it.

After thinking for a short while in silence, Rem offered a rebuttal:

"...Last night, I had a conversation with Shera. A conversation about what her dreams were... and what our future together would be like."

"She probably thought talking about that would make you happy or something."

"...But what would be the point of that? Not to mention she left without so much as a word to me."

"The more friendly you are with someone, the harder it is to say goodbye, right?"

"...Did it seem like she felt that way?"

"......... No..."

Diablo thought back to his conversation with Shera—

"Are you not going to say goodbye to Rem?"

"Never mind that, I have to hurry it up and get home with my big brother."

—*"Never mind that"*?

Something— No, some *things* had felt out of place about her. He would run out of fingers if he tried to count them all on both hands... But the number of times he had grown distant with others without noticing was still greater.

"At any rate, it just isn't possible..." Rem repeated. "I can only think that someone used some kind of magic on her."

"Maybe something happened that she didn't like."

As he stayed lying down, Rem came at Diablo with more questions.

"Are you sure there wasn't something off about the way Shera spoke? Can you say with absolute certainty that she wasn't under the control of some kind of spell?"

He couldn't; but that kind of magic shouldn't exist in the first place. He had already memorized all the spells and treasures implemented in Cross Reverie, and even cleared all the story quests as well.

"There was a treasure…. that could give you control over other people."

"What!?" Rem bolted upright.

"But it wasn't a flute… And it was obvious to see which NPCs were being controlled. They would talk in a stilted, stiff way…"

"…What are you talking about?"

"For there to be something in this world that could make the person under control talk so normally…"

"…Doesn't that mean it is possible something like that could exist? The Elves have inherited a majority of treasures from the Celestials. And at the risk of sounding rude… Well, it wouldn't be strange for them to have things that even you are not aware of, Diablo."

"That's just cheating…"

—Cheating?

It would break the game if it actually existed. Players would definitely bash it as a crap quest.

—But this world is different from the game. Can I definitely say something like that doesn't exist?

Shera really was being controlled by magic— Coming to that conclusion made all his past mistakes come rushing back to him, making him feel a pain in his chest.

(A convenient perversion of the truth.)

(The miserable delusions of someone who has been abandoned.)

(Unrelenting, lingering regret.)

—Disgusting.

These things were already ingrained in his body, to an almost sickening degree.

—*It would have been better if I wasn't summoned with just the looks and abilities of a Demon Lord, but if I had become the "Demon Lord, Diablo" down to the very core of my being— not just an act...*

I was rejected once. I'm tired of chasing after others just to be rejected again.

...But the energy to get himself up never came.

"I... I will respect her will."

Rem let out a sigh.

—*I disappointed her... That's fine, too. I'm sure Rem would have distanced herself from me someday, might as well be now.*

Rem stood up from the bed.

"...I believe in Shera. Even if it isn't magic, it must be some kind of lapse in judgment on her part."

—*Why are you going that far? You could get rejected again, making the pain even worse.*

It was a mystery to him.

Rem stared at him intently. Then, she spoke deliberately:

"It's because I'm her friend."

Her voice penetrated deep inside him.

He swallowed the negative comments he had been on the verge of saying as Rem headed towards the doorway.

—*Friend...*

I feel like Shera was the first one to say it like that...

He took a deep breath— It was a strange feeling, like it was the first time in a long while he had gotten some fresh air into his lungs.

"Wait, Rem."

"…Are you going to stop me?" She turned to look at him with a stern expression.

"You aren't thinking about trying to get into the Elf encampment by yourself… Are you?"

A bold smile crept onto Diablo's face.

"…W-Well…" Rem looked at the ground. "If I was only there to see Shera, I would think they would not get in my way."

"Are you sure about that?"

"…No. I already know that they will try and interfere… and I know that I may not come back alive. According to my intuition, Shera is being controlled by some kind of magic. If that is true, Prince Keera will most certainly try to stop me."

"What will you do if they get in your way?"

"…I will not give up until I meet with Shera. I am an Adventurer who is trying to defeat a Demon Lord. I do not give up so easily."

Her voice was determined.

Still smiling, Diablo got off the bed.

"You amuse me. You would go through all that trouble to meet with someone who left at their own will?"

"…Yes."

Diablo picked up the war scythe that was laid on the floor. It had felt heavy the first time he had held it; but right now, it felt lighter than ever.

He spread both his arms wide.

"To you, Rem Galleu, one of the beings who has summoned me… I ask you—"

Diablo unleashed the ultimate line, befitting of a Demon Lord:

"—Do you desire power? Do you yearn for the power of a Demon Lord!?"

Rem gave a wholehearted nod.

"Yes! I need your power, Demon Lord Diablo!"

"Very well; then you shall have it! To fulfill your desire, I shall bestow you with a glimpse of this overwhelming power of mine!"

†

When they had left the room, Alicia was waiting for them in the hallway. The war scythe resting on his shoulder, along with Tenma's Staff and the potions he had made earlier stuffed inside his pouch, Diablo attempted to step around her.

"Sir Diablo, though it may seem rude, I heard your conversation just now." Alicia's voice was firm.

"And?"

"I understand how you feel. However, Princess Shera has made her intentions clear and left Faltra of her own accord. Even if it is just to see her, we are talking about the princess of another country… This could serve as a trigger for war!"

"Oh hoh, simply by me going to visit her?"

"There is the possibility that your actions could cause you to be treated as a criminal by both the Human and Elven countries!"

Alicia's voice was desperate.

At this rate, Diablo and Rem would be labeled as criminals. Perhaps Alicia had put forth the idea in an attempt to deter them from going ahead with their plans.

And yet, Diablo still shook his head.

"Shera could be under the influence of magic, you see."

"Th-That's… If you could prove that… then even if the perpetrator was the leader of a country, they would not be able to avoid the ramifications. But even then, there is no guarantee that you would not be charged with some sort of crime...!!"

"That isn't the case, Alicia."

"What?"

"If Shera is under the influence of magic, there's someone here who wants to free her from that."

Alicia looked at Rem. Keeping her mouth drawn tight, Rem nodded.

"...I'm sorry, but I'm going to go and make Shera come to her senses."

"Y-You can't! Are you planning on making Humans and Elves— No, the entire world your enemy!?" Alicia's voice was laced with panic.

A fiendish smile came onto Diablo's face.

"Alicia, who do you think I am? I go wherever I want, do whatever I please... and no one will be able to stop me."

"But if you are to head out to meet the Elves, the governor is sure to notice! If he feels that what you are doing is ill-advised, I would think there is a high possibility he will send the army to stop you."

—*Oh yeah, the governor had sent "Observers" to follow us around, huh.*

Diablo hadn't been able to detect their presence whatsoever. Just through their superior surveillance skills, he could tell that Galford's soldiers were extremely well-trained.

But Diablo's feelings were firm.

"Hmph... If they try to get in my way, then that means I will have to raze the governor's soldiers first."

"I don't believe it..." Alicia said, staggering backwards.

"Miss Rem, are you truly all right with this!? You will lose not only your achievements as an Adventurer, but your life in this town as well!"

"...I simply do not feel right without confirming Shera's true feelings myself. I do not think what she said to me was a lie... If her words are being distorted by magic, then I want to save her. And, um... Having no one to save you is truly painful."

"We are going. If you are going to try and stop us, I have no qualms fighting you. However, we are in a hurry, so don't expect me to go easy on you."

Leaving Alicia behind, Diablo and Rem continued down the hallway.

Alicia circled around, standing in front of them.

—*Is she actually planning on fighting us!?*

"If that is the case... will you please allow me to accompany you?"

"What? Are you actually insane?"

In a panic, Rem attempted to stop her.

"What are you saying, Alicia!? Our situations are completely different than yours! From the beginning, we were Adventurers who never relied on the country for anything; but you are an Imperial Knight! It is unthinkable for you to abandon your position like this!"

From here on out, Diablo and Rem could end up becoming criminals. That was because they thought of Shera as their friend; that's what they believed. But Alicia was someone they had just met. They had no bonds that held them together, and she owed them no favors.

"It was not like I wanted to become an Imperial Knight," Alicia said, shaking her head. "Rather, I wanted to be able to help those who needed it. I am still not convinced about what happened with

Miss Shera. Not only that, but I cannot leave you alone either, Miss Rem."

"...You said that before, didn't you. But I do not think it is worth throwing away your position as an Imperial Knight."

"If you put it that way, then I could say the same for you throwing away your life as an Adventurer."

"...I see. Then I have nothing I can say in response to that. If Diablo says it is all right, then I cannot stop you."

He was conflicted. Being an Adventurer meant living life on a day-by-day basis, where you could end up spending who knows how many days in a dungeon. But on the other hand, was it okay to get Alicia, an Imperial Knight who barely knew Shera, involved as well?

—*Well, I guess it's up to the person themselves to decide the value of something.*

If she said she wanted to prioritize saving Shera over her own position as an Imperial Knight, then Diablo and Rem couldn't change how she felt about that. In fact, he appreciated it.

"Alicia, are you positive you will not end up regretting this?"

An earnest expression on her face, she nodded.

"Of course. Not to mention, though it may seem rude, it would probably take the two of you a decent amount of time to locate the Elf encampment. I have already asked about the specific location of Prince Keera and his soldiers."

"Oh hoh? From the governor?"

"Yes. What do you say? I don't think there is any harm in bringing me along, do you?"

It's true, she would be useful.

Diablo couldn't care less about Keera, but wherever he was, Shera was probably there, too. Walking around the forest near the Eastern Lakefront looking for them would be rough. Also, since

Shera might be there as well, he couldn't just start firing off his most powerful spells there, either. Having Shera taken back to the Kingdom of Greenwood afterwards just because they had taken too much time would only lead to even more trouble.

Judging from what he had seen of Keera's personality, he should show himself if Diablo taunted him openly— Is what he had been thinking, but if they knew where the troops were located, that made everything a whole lot easier.

"Hmph… Even though I said you do not have to try and be useful… You seem to like making things hard on yourself, don't you?"

"Yes, I'm told that a lot."

Rem took Alicia's hand.

"Alicia, thank you!"

"Not at all. Let's do our best to save Shera. She must be under the control of some kind of magic, and suffering because of it."

†

The 《Eastern Lakefront Forest》—

A forest found on the eastern side of Seplia Lake, it was located to the southeast of the city of Faltra. The dark green foliage of the trees grew thick there.

Following Alicia's directions carefully, the group made their way through this ominous place.

In Cross Reverie, monsters would appear with relative frequency in the Eastern Lakefront Forest. Diablo remembered that the forest itself was always crawling with vicious beasts.

In game terms, though, this was still one of the beginning areas. The recommended level for this area was around 40. It was a place for players who had made their way to Faltra to grind levels and gain experience before heading to the Demon Lord's Domain. But Diablo couldn't sense any living creature around them; wild beasts were more sensitive to danger than the other races, so they probably noticed that the Elves were here and ran off.

It didn't exist in this world, but in the game, there was a radar that showed the map of the area and all living things around you. However, those using "Stealth" skills wouldn't appear on the radar. "Sensing a presence" in this world could be the equivalent of having the radar from the game. In that regard, it felt like the Elves were close, but he couldn't actually sense their presence.

It was just past noon, and right when Diablo was starting to think they should have brought some lunch or something—

Alicia suddenly stopped. She was staring intently at the multitude of tall tree trunks in front of them.

Diablo followed her gaze to where she was looking. The trees looked fuzzy and out of focus, with nothing about them standing out in particular. All he could make out of them was triangular shapes with a line down the middle, as if they had been cut out with a knife.

Turning around, Alicia spoke in a whisper:

"It seems like this is the place."

"...What should we do?" Rem whispered back. "I would think trying to sneak past the Elves and reaching Shera without them noticing would be quite difficult."

"Hmph..." Diablo snorted. "What are you saying? Why must we stand about whispering like this when we have merely come to pay Shera a visit?"

"...But will they actually let us see her?"

Rem was expecting the Elves to not let them see Shera; Diablo felt the same.

But if they wouldn't allow the group to see her, then on top of Shera's sudden change of heart, the Elves were basically saying, "She is being controlled by magic." It was a bit of reckless reasoning on their part—but it was enough to make them give it their all.

Not only that, but there was no time to spare. Elves specialized in Sneak skills, while Diablo's group did not. Even if they tried to move forward while staying hidden, they would be found out. If that was the case—

Taking a deep breath, Diablo shouted out:

"Attention, Elves! We know you're there! If you do not come out of that forest, I'll *burn* you out!"

The surrounding trees started to sway. And then—

Far away, ten Elves dropped out of the treetops, bows on their backs.

But that wasn't all. One after the other, Elves came pouring out of the forest.

—*Twenty, thirty, forty, fifty…*

They all wore green clothing that blended in with the trees. To be honest, Diablo wasn't confident that he could count them all accurately—but there were over one hundred of them at the very least. Maybe even two hundred. There were far more than the governor had predicted. If this were Cross Reverie, having this many characters on screen at once would be enough to make the game lag hard. Diablo had never taken on this many opponents at once before.

Keeping Rem and Alicia behind him, Diablo glared at the Elf army. He recognized one of the Elves standing at the vanguard of the troops: he was a young man who had been part of the elite Elf squad that had laid in wait in the Man-Eating Forest to try and take Shera back home.

If I remember right—

"Your name is Celsior, is it not?"

"Y-Yes… I'm honored you remembered." A nervous expression on his face, Celsior stepped forward.

"I want to meet with Shera. Lead me to her."

Diablo had made his demand clear.

"I cannot do that. Prince Keera has ordered us not to let anyone through here."

—As I thought.

Celsior's words served as the evidence needed to support their theory. Shera was being controlled by some kind of magic unknown to Diablo.

Rem's breath caught in her throat.

"Unforgivable," Alicia muttered.

Diablo asked another question; he didn't feel like wasting any more time.

"Shera is being controlled by magic, then. Is it that flute?"

Celsior had an anguished expression on his face, and yet—

"I cannot answer that!" An adamant refusal.

He looked like the type of person who would never lie; judging by his expression, tone of voice, and his eye contact, he was telling the truth.

Diablo made his rage known.

"You know, and yet you still follow his orders!? Do you truly believe that fool becoming king is for the good of your country, even though you realize he is controlling Shera with magic!?"

"The future of the Elves will be decided by our king! Our king-to-be, Prince Keera, has decided upon having a child with Princess

Shera for the benefit of our country. All we have to do is believe in the prosperity the future will bring and follow our king... Otherwise, our country will be torn apart!"

"Using *their* position as an excuse to throw away *your* ability to differentiate between good and evil is nothing short of being a slave, you *imbecile!*" Diablo roared.

"Th-This is for the sake of our country!"

Celsior readied his bow; one after the other, the rest of the Elves did the same.

Diablo heard the sound of countless bowstrings being drawn taut— Two hundred arrowheads were pointed towards him all at once.

"Stay behind me," Diablo told Rem and Alicia.

"Sir Diablo, there is no way to guard against so many arrows!"

"...Do not worry, just let him handle it. I may be scared right now... but even more than that, I believe in Diablo."

Diablo raised his war scythe.

"For the sake of your country, you say... You have made a grave mistake, Celsior! It is not the prince's wrath you should worry of; it is mine!"

"Fire!!" Celsior yelled.

Two hundred arrows blotted out the sky, pouring down like black rain.

Diablo held his left hand aloft as he cast his spell:

"《Volcanic Wall》!"

The earth in front of him erupted, spewing flames that reached heights beyond that of the trees in the forest, almost seeming to reach the sky itself.

The Elves screamed in horror as their arrows disintegrated to ash in the face of a spell reminiscent of a natural disaster. The surrounding trees were lit aflame, and everything was blown away. The area of forest in front of Diablo and the others that had once blocked their vision was now transformed to scorched rock and earth.

—Hmm… This spell does quite a lot of damage to the terrain itself.

It was a level 80 Earth and Fire-type magic that caused a wall of fire to erupt from the ground. It activated quickly, and was easy to use as a shield of sorts. The attack headed straight upwards, so its effective area was smaller than Diablo had expected.

As the air shimmered with heat waves, Celsior's face was contorted in terror.

"…It can't be… Impossible!"

"I have even more powerful spells that could have burned you all to ash, but the risk of losing my guides to show me the way to Shera would just end up being troublesome for me."

"Ngh… It's true, you may be strong… but don't underestimate the Elves!"

"Hm?"

"Behind you!" Rem shouted, while Alicia drew her sword.

—From behind!?

The Elves within the forest displayed extremely prominent Stealth skills. For a Demon Sorcerer such as Diablo, detecting traps or people lying in ambush wasn't his forte. Because of this, he hadn't been able to sense the enemies who were sneaking up directly behind him.

An Elf Warrior rushed in wielding a dagger, but Alicia caught it, deflecting it with her sword.

"I will not let you approach Sir Diablo!"

"Grk!?"

Blood splattered everywhere as she slashed into the Elf's shoulder.

At the same time, Rem threw out her crystals.

"Come forth, Asulau and Stoneman!"

A gigantic bull with three horns on its head came into existence. In addition, an enormous stone statue appeared as well. Though there was no face or eyes to be found on its square-shaped head, it felt like it was glaring at the Elves.

Though Rem may have been a Summoner, she was also a Pantherian who could fight in close-quarters using her natural agility. Though this only meant their three-on-two hundred brawl had turned into a five-on-two hundred skirmish...

Diablo's group had more shields now. When fighting against opponents like these, where Diablo's group didn't know where their next attacks would be coming from, this was their boon.

—*Summons are more useful than I imagined.*

Diablo forged ahead. With every step he took forward, the more the Elves moved one back. He had already burnt any trees the Elves could have hidden themselves to a crisp.

"Hmph… If you wish to throw your lives away for the sake of a foolish prince, then come face me!"

Several of the Elves ran away on the spot, but there were still several Elves who came charging at him, however.

It was hard to restrain himself knowing that Shera was just ahead of him.

Location: Inside a tent where its fabric was suspended by tree branches.

There were several boxes decorated with extravagant ornaments there, as well as a circular table and a chair. A carpet was spread out along the ground; on it sat the Elf Princess, Shera—a blank expression on her face.

A slight distance away, propping himself up against one of the tent's support poles while playing a flute—was the Elf Prince, Keera. His eyes flashed, and a purple light started to gather around Shera: it was the light of a spell.

The expression on Shera's face twisted.

"Ahhhh…"

Taking the flute from his lips, Keera sneered.

"Heh heh heh… 'Overwrite: Shera will answer any question I ask her.'"

"Ngh… Nnnnnnnngh…"

Shera's anguish slowly subsided, eventually returning to the vague expression she had on her face from before.

"How about it, Shera? Feel like answering my questions?"

"Yes… Ask anything you like."

"What did that Diablo guy demand of you? What did he order you to do? Not knowing that just pisses me off. Say it… I'll have you do the same and *more* using 'Overwrite'!"

"Um… Orders?" Shera looked confused.

"He used that collar to give you orders, didn't he? He had to have been lying when he said he didn't."

"Hm… Oh, yeah… He did."

"Ha! As I thought!"

"He said to 'shake hands with Rem, and with a smile,'" Shera said, embarrassed.

"…What."

"Haha… We were fighting over Diablo back then…"

BAM! Keera slammed his fist against a nearby tree trunk.

"Not things like that, you idiot!"

"But he didn't order me to do anything else!"

"So he wasn't lying… Damn it."

Right then, far off in the distance—a sound similar to an explosion.

"Hm? Did some kind of beast show up or something? Even though they're supposed to be elites, they're having that hard a time with a few weaklings… I'll have to punish them after this is over," Keera said, his words laced with venom.

Shera stared in the direction the sound had come from. Her chest started to feel warmer.

"…Could it be…? No, of course not… I did something awful…"

"Hey, Shera, here's the next one: 'Overwrite: Shera cannot move.'"

"Huh!? Ngh!? Hngg…!?"

Shera's voice was tainted with anguish once more.

"Hehe… No squirming around now, got it?"

Keera grabbed both of Shera's hands and threw a pair of handcuffs on her that had been hanging on an adjacent tree branch.

"What are you doing!?"

"Watch, and you'll see soon enough. After all, you can't move, so that's about all you *can* do."

Saying that, Keera kicked over a large pot lying at his feet. It toppled over, the lid coming undone, and a viscous mucus oozing out from the inside. This wasn't just *any* kind of mucus, however— It squirmed as it moved.

"Eek!?"

Shera screamed, but with her arms suspended in the air by her wrists, she wasn't able to move.

"Hah! No need to get so scared," Keera snickered. "It's just a Slime."

"N-No! It's gonna melt me and eat me!"

"If it was one of the carnivorous types, it would. This guy only eats fabrics."

With a sizzling sound, the carpet started to dissolve away. The expression on Shera's face stiffened.

"I don't want that either! Go away!"

"If you don't like it, then just run away. Those handcuffs aren't locked."

"Nghhh... I want to run away... But I can't move... Wh-Why? What's happening to me!?"

Keera put the flute back into the sash around his waist, grabbing a bottle of some kind of alcohol instead. Using his teeth to remove the cork, he spat it out and began guzzling down the contents of the bottle.

The slime advanced on Shera. Dissolving the carpet as it moved, it slowly came closer...

"Eek! No, don't come near me!"

Its movements were slow, but Shera could not move.

The slime started to wrap around her boots. It was so hot that the tips of her toes heated up, and the top of her boots started to dissolve. The slime entered her shoes, making contact with her skin.

"Nooooooo!!"

The slime was lukewarm; it was a sensation like being licked by a giant tongue.

The shoes that once covered her feet melted away. It left the metal and leather behind, showing that it really did only eat fabric. The sickening feeling of a tongue crawling over her skin made its way from her ankles towards her knees.

"Ah! N-No! What!?"

The moment it touched the back of her leg, it sent a jolt up her spine, making her shudder.

Shera couldn't move of her own accord— It was almost as if she didn't want to move. Even though she wanted to run away, the thought of "not wanting to move" completely overtook everything else in her mind.

Continuing to down his drink, Keera laughed as he watched her.

"Ha-hah! So you like it on the back of your legs, you lewd, lewd girl!"

"Wh-What are you saying!? This feels completely gross!"

Finally, the Slime had made its way up to her thighs, then wrapped itself around her waist. She was overtaken by a sensation she had never felt on the lower parts of her body before, making the rest of her body start to go limp.

"Fwah… Nrgh…"

She gritted her teeth. Her breathing sounded strange, but she absolutely didn't want Keera to hear her voice now.

"Mmmph! Nrrrrrrgh!"

"Haha… You sure are putting up a fight, aren't you. I'll join you once I finish drinking this. I'm sure you'll be good and ready by then."

"Nghhh! Mnnn! —Ahh… Keera…"

"Yes?"

"I…hate you…"

"Ha! I already knew that. Don't piss me off now, it'll only make me want to kill you before we make a successor."

"I'd rather you kill me than do that!"

"After all, I bet you think it, too— That it would have been better if I had been eaten by those monsters instead of our big brother, is that it!?"

"I don't know what you're talking about! Our older brother died before I was even born!"

The Slime had wrapped itself around Shera's entire body. It had made it all the way up to her chest, wrapping itself around her arms as well. She couldn't move now even if she wanted to; it was like she had sunk into a pit of mud.

This lukewarm, soft, squirming mass was crawling over her skin. It stimulated her thighs, her bottom, her back, and a host of other places on her body. The feeling made Shera's breath catch in her throat, sending convulsions throughout the muscles in her back.

"Gnh—ngh! Mnnn! Hrg! Ah—ahhhn!!"

Shera's green clothes were turned to foam by the semi-translucent Slime, with her undergarments now exposed. She thought she would die from the shame.

"N-No… Stop… Stop it…" Tears dripped from her cheeks.

Shera knew that, even if she called for Diablo, there was no chance of him coming. After all, she was the one who had left the group after saying all those terrible things to him.

But even so, Shera cried out the Demon Lord's name.

The side of the tent ripped open—

Chapter 3 Going to War

Diablo tore through the tent using his war scythe. The blade did not glide smoothly through it, but rather ripped it to shreds.

Shera was there: bound by handcuffs, a Slime enveloping her up to the chest, and her skin exposed.

Diablo's anger surged from his body. This anger was no act; it was an intent to kill.

The Slime that had entwined itself around Shera fell off her like spilling water, fleeing deeper inside the tent.

Now free of the Slime, all of Shera's strength left her. The handcuffs around her wrists creaked as they supported her weight. Gasping for breath, Shera looked towards him.

"……Diablo? Is this real…? This isn't a dream?"

"Did I keep you waiting, Shera?"

Diablo stepped inside, making his way towards Shera. Rem and Alicia followed after him, their breath catching in their throats upon seeing Shera. They turned to look at the tent's other occupant— Keera—their eyes smoldering in anger.

"…How dare you do such a thing!"

"Prince Keera… Even if you are royalty, this is something you cannot be forgiven for!"

"And just what the hell are *you* all doing!? Barging in on the prince's official duties like this… Do you *want* to go to war? Or you want to die, is that it? What the hell are you thinking?"

His back leaning against a tree trunk, Keera threw his bottle of booze to the ground.

Diablo glared at Keera, eyes brimming with resentment.

"...'Official duties'?"

"That's right. It's my *very* important duty to make sure that the royal lineage does not die out."

"That's what you call stringing her up with handcuffs and putting a Slime on her!?"

"Just a little foreplay. No matter if you're a guy or gal, it's much better heating things up like this, don't you think?"

"I was wrong after all... Even if it meant turning the town into a sea of flames, I shouldn't have let Shera go back then."

Stepping towards Shera, he removed the handcuffs from her wrists. "I'm sorry I was late."

"Diablo... You actually... came for me...?"

The look on Shera's face said she still couldn't believe it.

"Please, use this." Alicia handed Diablo her cape.

He covered the half-naked Shera with the crimson cape. Tears dropped from her face.

"Thank... you... Thank you..."

Seeing this, Keera let out a resentful sigh.

"Damn... Even though I went through the trouble of having those elite squads of Elves around, they didn't even notice these intruders... They're more useless than I thought. I'm going to have to punish them all for this!"

It seemed the prince was under the impression Diablo and the others had managed to sneak by the guards unnoticed.

"Did you not hear what was happening outside?" Diablo challenged.

With the magic I used back there, the noise alone should have been pretty loud...

"Oh, I heard it all right. You sure are idiots, making that much noise... It might be for the best if you just turned tail and ran now. The elite squadrons of Elves are sure to have noticed that, and should be here any second."

Keera's shoulders shook as he snickered at them.

"So you still believe you can utilize your little Elf squad. Well, I'm sure that must seem like common sense to you."

"What?"

"Why don't you go outside and see for yourself."

His face shrouded in doubt, Keera stuck his head out of the tent:

The forest was engulfed in flames.

Masses of Elves could be seen, injured and moaning in pain. Some were healing their comrades; others holding their knees in a fetal position; and others had broken down crying.

They had surely seen Diablo enter the prince's tent. The Elves had followed the enemy all the way there—

But now, none of the Elves stood up to stop him. They had lost their will to fight.

Practically hysteric, Keera screamed.

"GODDAMNIT!! Why the hell did they go and get destroyed like that!? Not to mention this is an international problem now! There's absolutely going to be war!"

"I'm only here to confirm whether Shera truly wishes to return or not," Diablo answered back.

"There's no way a Demon like you could meet with the Elf princess! What the hell kind of reason is that!"

"So, you have resorted to controlling Shera using underhanded tactics…"

"Wh-Wh-What!?" Keera flinched, and started to shake. "Where's your proof!? Are you saying you have proof!?"

"I don't need proof. Once I ask how Shera really feels about this, then *this* will all be over."

"Oh, I see… So you don't have any proof, do you?" The composure returned to Keera's face. "Then hurry up and get lost. I'll make an official complaint of this to the Lyferian Kingdom!"

—*I don't know what he's done to her…*

But it seems like he still thinks he can weasel his way out of this.

"Once I hear Shera's true intentions, I will leave."

"And *I'm* telling you, Shera decided to come back here all on her own. She's my property! She's finally come to realize her duties as princess of the Elves; that's why she came back! How do you not understand that?"

Getting nastier with every word, Keera gave an order: "Hey, Shera! Say it! What is it you have to do!?"

Shera, who'd just had tears streaming down her face, suddenly went back to that strange expression. She wasn't smiling, nor was she crying; it was a vague, normal expression. If it were any other situation, then there wouldn't be anything strange about this expression… But right now, it could only be thought of as strange.

"I have to go back. The Kingdom of Greenwood is my home, after all. If I don't make a successor with my brother, then the royal line will die out. Keeping the royal family going is much more important than my own freedom."

These repeated words were nothing but unnatural in this situation.

The expression on Rem and Alicia's faces stiffened. With this, there could be no more doubt: Diablo was enraged.

Keera was the only one laughing.

"Puhaha! You heard her! There, you satisfied now!? Now get lost!"

—It's pretty much a Geass.

Not only that, but it wasn't easy to tell that the person was being controlled; almost sickeningly so. As far as Diablo knew, this kind of magic did not exist in Cross Reverie. He had seen examples of it in other mediums, and he had even heard that brainwashing existed in real-life as well.

—To think this stuff existed in other worlds, too!

Now that I think about it, the slavery system didn't exist in the game either. The devs must have removed any content not suitable for children from the game.

"I will shatter that vile magic of yours."

"Hey! Weren't we supposed to respect Shera's will here!? What the hell!?"

Diablo pointed his war scythe at the enraged Keera.

"I plan to do just that. This will be it… I will make this the most complete and fair way to ask how she feels."

There was only one thing to do. Turning towards Shera, he shouted:

"I command you, as master of the Enslavement Collar you bear! Shera, speak now your true feelings! You are not bound by any magic, so reveal what lies in the depths of your own heart!"

The light returned to Shera's eyes.

She looked at her surroundings—
She looked at the palms of her hands—
Slowly, still shaking, her lips moved:
"I… I want…"
Tears rained from her eyes.

"I want to be free! I want to be with Rem and Diablo…!!"

Diablo pulled Shera close to him. Shera wrapped her arms around him as well.

Rem pointed the metal claws covering her hand at Keera.

"…What you have done was unforgivably foolish. You deserve a punishment befitting of your actions."

Alicia placed a hand on her sword. "Despite your status as royalty, this is an obvious crime!"

"What the hell is wrong with you all!" Keera howled. "Useless, useless, useless, useless! You're all so useless! Don't piss me off like this! Is there something wrong with your damn heads!?"

"Can you tell us everything?" Diablo asked. "What did he do to you in those five minutes at the inn?"

"Yeah, I can… I told him that I wasn't coming back. But he didn't believe it, and said that I could have been forced to say it because of the enslavement collar. Then he said he would use a spell that would remove any orders placed on me…"

"And you actually believed that?"

—Shera might be a little too easy to fool in that regard. Though how trusting she is of other people is kind of endearing.

"He used his fingers… to draw something on my forehead… And then everything got fuzzy once he played his flute… That's right, he said something to me. Something about 'Overwrite,' and that the

225

next time I heard the flute, I was supposed to say that I would go back home with him for the sake of the country… and then to forget that he had said all this to me…"

"An obvious use of magic on his part."

Diablo held Shera tight. Her shoulders were trembling.

Keera kicked the pot that had been lying on the floor, smashing it in grand fashion.

"Whaaaaaaaat!? What the hell is this! It's already over! You think you can just waltz in here and ruin everything like this!? I won't stand for it! This is an injustice!"

Diablo put Shera in Rem's care. "I leave her to you."

"Of course… Shera, can you walk?"

"Y-Yeah… I'm fine."

Alicia had tried to make Keera realize the truth of the matter, but with the current situation, he was having none of it.

—*He may even get violent.*

"You deserve to be judged." Diablo gripped his scythe.

"Grk…!? O-Oh, I see! I see it now! So that's how it is! Now you bastards are aiming for the Kingdom of Greenwood! You used Shera to lure me out and finish me off, is that it!? That's dirty, you damn Humans!"

"Why!?" Keera scratched furiously at his head. "Why don't things go the way I want them to!? You pieces of shit! This isn't fun at all! What is the meaning of this, having these ignorant commoners piss me off so much!?"

The prince kicked over the desk and various boxes, thoroughly trashing the place. It was all his own possessions, so Diablo had no qualms about it.

There was no reason to hang around here any longer.

"Prince Keera," Alicia declared, "I am placing you under arrest."

Diablo had only just noticed it now, but Keera had managed to pick up a jeweled case amongst the many other objects he had scattered throughout the tent. Inside the case was a gem that gleamed with an eerie, multicolored glow, as if it were covered in an oily membrane. It was enormous.

Keera looked at Diablo and the others, a wild grin on his face.

"That's enough… I have had *enough!* It's the death penalty for all of you!!"

"Keera!? You can't! Not that Summon!" Shera shouted out in a panic.

—*A Summon!? That huge jewel is supposed to be a Summon crystal!?*

"The treasures of the Elves can destroy the world itself! If this world won't entertain me, then it should just cease to exist!"

Diablo made Rem and the others get back. He stood at the ready with his war scythe.

"Very well! If you decided to challenge me—Then I shall grant you the retribution you so deserve!"

"You're the *first* to die, Demon! Get out here, 《Force Hydra》!"

He smashed the rainbow-colored jewel against the ground, shattering it to pieces—

And from that ominously colored treasure, a Summon manifested into existence.

†

A species of Dragon; a monster with four heads— And it was gargantuan.

It burst through the tent like it was made of tissue paper, and its heads far surpassed any of the surrounding trees in size. Its body was covered in scales with spots of blue, red, and green on them. They were covered in a kind of viscous mucus, and sparkled brightly.

Taking Shera with them, Diablo and the others moved away from the tent. If they stayed too close, it was likely they would have been stomped to death; but everyone had made it away unharmed.

They could hear the screams of the Elves who had lost their will to fight: some were fleeing; some had broken down laughing; others were pleading with Keera to restrain the Summon.

Ignoring them all, Keera looked up at the Summon, an expression of pure ecstasy on his face

"It's wonderful, isn't it! Just as I would expect from the forbidden Summon said to possess the ability to send the whole world to its demise! Look at its magnificence! —Its power! —Its divine appearance!"

—Divine is the last word I would think to describe it.

If Diablo was being completely honest, its appearance screamed "sinister" more than anything else.

—I've never seen a Summon that looked like this before.

I could have just forgotten about it, but did this guy show up in the game? There are monsters out there the size of hills, so I wouldn't say it's the most powerful thing I've ever seen… But if this were the game, even if I tried to put some distance between us, parts of it would still stretch beyond the corner of the screen.

At the very least, it was definitely the largest monster he had fought since coming to this world. Since he had always been on the other side of a monitor, he had never been able to experience it himself… Yet there was an almost overwhelming intensity to looking up at the monster like this.

Diablo froze in place. Dragons were generally tenacious enemies, covered in nigh impenetrable scales…

—Can I win against this thing?

Taken away by Rem and the others, Shera called out from a distance:

"We should run! That Summon's been passed down for generations in the royal family— There's no way to stop it; it's said to be undefeatable! There's no way even my brother will be able to control it!"

So that's why they say it can "destroy the world"—

Now it all added up. It seemed like a fairly strong Summon, and Keera didn't appear to be a high-level Summoner; but if this thing was one of the Elf's treasures, then that would certainly explain it. So even if you weren't a Summoner, this was an item that anyone could use— Even, for example, someone from the Elven royal family.

There were no treasures in the game that could call forth a Summon, and the same went for the flute that had controlled Shera. It seemed like the Elf's treasures hadn't been implemented in the game. Even though Cross Reverie was a game that was updated weekly and monthly, with new gameplay elements being added all the time, this world had things that didn't quite exist in-game yet. It seemed Diablo had found himself in a version of Cross Reverie that ignored any ethical limitations, and where anything and everything was implemented. Thinking of it that way filled him with excitement, in a way.

According to what Shera had said, this thing couldn't be controlled. But with Keera's shouts of "Get them, Force Hydra! Kill them all!" it seemed he was giving orders to it as if it were his own Summon. And right when Diablo thought Keera was actually controlling it—

Keera was almost crushed by the Summon's tail.

—That's what you get for standing so close to it.

As Keera ran away, the Force Hydra had started its rampage with complete disregard for the prince.

—*So he really isn't in control of that thing... How in the world does he think that Summon is his to command in a situation like that?*

No use thinking about it now— Let's beat this thing before any more casualties appear.

"I'm going to destroy it!" Diablo called out towards Rem and the others. "You don't mind that, right, Shera?"

"You can do that!?"

"Of course!"

"...There is no need to worry about us." Rem nodded. "I will make sure Shera does not do any *other* stupid things."

"You're still calling me stupid, even at a time like this!?"

"...You would actually have to be stupid to make me worry that much about you."

"You were worried about me! Thank you, Rem!"

Shera threw herself around Rem. Though she pushed against Shera's shoulders as if she didn't like it, Rem made no attempt to get away from her.

Alicia unsheathed her sword and gave a salute: "I will protect them, even if it costs me my life!"

"Good. Get back so you don't get caught up in my magic. I'm sure this thing will come at us using long-distance attacks as well."

"U-Understood!"

Diablo stood in front of the Force Hydra; its multiple heads were thick and stout. Looking at it up close like this, it truly was enormous— It seemed there was no need to hold back.

He stabbed the blade of his scythe into the ground. Reaching into his pouch, he produced Tenma's Staff.

"Hahahahaha! You idiot, there's no way you can win!" Keera had a twisted smile on his face. "Just you existing stresses me out, so hurry up and die, Demon!"

Though Keera couldn't control the Summon, it seemed he still had absolute confidence in its power.

Diablo, on the other hand, had already used up a large chunk of his MP fighting with the Elf soldiers from earlier.

I should end this as quickly as possible...

He raised his staff:

"《Heaven's Fall》!"

A multitude of rocks appeared in the sky. This was an Earth spell learned at level 100 that would spawn a seemingly infinite number of meteorites and deal damage to a wide area.

Using first-person view, it was possible to guide the rocks towards your target; the AoE would be smaller, but the attack would be much more powerful. It was a hard spell to use on smaller opponents, but extremely effective against large monsters.

Diablo swung his staff downwards— With the sound of rushing wind, countless meteorites sliced through the air and rained down upon the Force Hydra. The violent impact made the ground tremble and trees shake with a tremendous sound.

Clouds of dust were thrown up in the air; before long, their visions cleared—

The Force Hydra had lost one of its four heads.

—This thing is weaker than I expected. I can probably beat it if I hit it with four or five more volleys...

...Now we wait to see how it retaliates.

Just as he finished making his assessment—

Suddenly, the head the Hydra had lost grew back out of its neck stump.

—It regenerated!? That was way too fast! What is this, a bug!?

There were some monsters that would partially regenerate in the middle of battle, but this was the first time he had seen it happen so quickly.

The regenerated head spewed forth a green stream of air from its mouth.

—A Wind breath attack!?

Having let his guard down, Diablo took the attack head-on, being blown away in the process.

Dragon breath attacks were purely elemental. They were treated as neither physical or magical attacks. Because of that, Diablo's magic reflection and damage reducing abilities didn't activate. Though the same could be said of most fantasy RPGs, Dragons tended to receive favorable treatment from the devs when it came to skills in Cross Reverie.

The 《Wind Resistance》 skill would have come in handy here, but unfortunately, Diablo didn't have it.

I've figured out that the Force Hydra seems to have two skills: 《Regeneration》 and 《Wind Breath》— Diablo thought to himself.

Normally, Summons came with the limitation of having only one skill. Of course, that's not to say there weren't Summons that had special attributes, such as high defense or high attack.

—But the regeneration ability of this Force Hydra doesn't seem to be a skill. I think I can say for sure that it's some kind of special attribute: extremely high resilience.

That, or maybe this is a sign Cross Reverie would eventually implement Summons with multiple skills?

It seemed quite likely, considering it would buff the laughingstock that was the Summoner class in the game.

—It's also possible this world is only similar *to Cross Reverie, and that's it.*

Diablo pushed himself off the ground, standing up once more. The damage was nothing to sneeze at, but the only wounds he had were scratches, at best.

—Must have been cuts caused by that Wind breath attack.

It wasn't like he had lost a huge chunk of HP, but he did want to avoid continuing to take on these attacks.

As he was working to put some distance between himself and the Summon, Fire, Ice, and Sand breath attacks came surging out from the remaining three heads.

"This thing has five skills!?"

—I had thought it was around level 80 or so…

But it looks like it's over level 100. It's strong enough to stand equally with the monsters that show up in the Demon Lord's Domain. It might be even stronger than Edelgard, the Fallen commander I fought before.

Becoming full of himself, Keera shouted in a shrill voice:

"Good, that's good! *This* is my power! I don't need anyone getting in my way or holding me back!"

"Diablo!" Shera cried out. "There should be a core somewhere inside of it! If you can destroy that, it should go back to being a crystal!"

—I see. So that's how it is.

It was a common practice with boss monsters for there to be specific parts of the boss you needed to attack to damage it.

"Ha! For an idiot, you sure remember some useless things," Keera sneered. "However! This thing keeps its core moving throughout the inside of its body, and it's not as big as the crystal it came out of— There's no chance in hell someone like you would be able to find it!"

"Having it change its weak spot is normal for these creatures… Though I never intended to search for it in the first place."

"What!?"

The patterns and weak points for this type of monster were pretty much already written on the strategy Wiki. Diablo himself had even contributed info to it in the past. But when it came to actually facing these things for the first time, you had to go through some struggles before you could begin studying its patterns.

Diablo pressed the attack with his magic, destroying another of the hydra's heads; but just like before, it regenerated and retaliated with a breath attack. Taking it like before, Diablo kept accumulating damage.

"G-Go get him! Don't lose!" Shera shouted in a panic.

"...Is it really strong enough that Diablo can't win against it?" Rem said worriedly.

"Good...! This is great! I win!" Keera burst out laughing. "Keep going, just like that! Kill him!!"

"I see." Diablo nodded. "It has high stats, but is lacking in its mental capacities."

For the third time, he destroyed one of the Hydra's heads— And just like before, it promptly grew back. The regenerated head once again struck back at him with a Wind breath attack.

—This thing is leading its attacks on me, but I can outrun them with my high agility.

Diablo started charging a spell while avoiding the Force Hydra's three breath attacks: Fire, Ice, and Sand. It was a fixed pattern.

So basically, this guy has one skill:

"《Regeneration, followed by four breath attacks》— That's what its skill is. It may look strong, but its patterns are so predictable that it's useless in a fight against an actual person."

It might change its attack pattern depending on how much HP it lost, or if Diablo destroyed another one of its heads instead, but he didn't have time to confirm every single one of its patterns. There wasn't any site for him to compare info with other players to be found in this world, either.

Diablo confirmed his surroundings: none of the Elves, nor Alicia, Shera, or Rem, were in danger of being caught up in the spell.

He rapidly closed the distance between himself and the Force Hydra. Pointing Tenma's Staff towards the monster, he cast his spell:

"《Matoi Izuna》!!"

A condensed mass of lightning appeared from the tip of his staff, its appearance that of a sparkling orb, and sent it flying towards the Force Hydra. There was a small distance the attack had to travel first, but given the size of the Summon, there was no time or space for the monster to dodge it.

The instant the shining ball of light made contact with its target—

The Force Hydra's body started to quake— It spasmed continuously as lightning poured forth from its eyes and mouths.

Matoi Izuna was a combination Wind and Light elemental spell. By taking a vicious whirlwind and cloaking it with lighting, it would lodge itself inside the target, tearing it apart from the inside. In Cross Reverie, it would deal damage over time while locking the target in place; it would finish its assault by dealing massive damage.

"Tearing apart the target from the inside-out" was only the description for the spell in the game— But right now, he was seeing the effects with his own eyes.

As the hydra continued to convulse, white sparks starting to fly off of its electricity-wreathed body. Then, finally, the "massive damage" activated—

An explosion of pure white.

A pillar of light completely engulfed the Force Hydra. Rem and the others shielded their eyes, unable to stand the dazzling brightness.

Keera could only stare, dumbfounded.

"Wh… What…?"

The pillar of light disappeared. Where the Force Hydra once stood, there was now a hole in the earth, the bottom of which could not be seen. But it wasn't like the ground had split open—

It had been completely obliterated.

Along with the Force Hydra, the ground, the clouds above, and even the air itself where the Summon once was, had been entirely removed from this world.

—For some reason, Light-elemental spells always seem to make enemies turn into particles of light when they're defeated… It's pretty to watch, but also kind of brutal when you think about it…

"…What is happening here… I don't… get it…" Mouth agape, Keera stared at the area that had been obliterated by Diablo. He crumpled to his knees.

Rem and the other two girls came running over to Diablo.

"Diablo! You actually managed to defeat that powerful Summon!" Rem proclaimed. "Just what I would expect from a Demon Lord!"

Shera came bounding over.

"That was amazing! The Force Hydra is Greenwood's ace in the hole, something we're only supposed to use if our enemies reach the royal palace! It's supposed to be able to handle entire armies! How did you beat it by yourself!? You're so strong, Diablo!"

Alicia appeared to be shocked speechless.

Confirming that the girls were all safe, Diablo breathed a silent sigh of relief.

"I'm so glad you're all right"—is also something a Demon Lord would never say, so he said nothing at all.

"What the hell is with you? A-Aren't you supposed to be a Demon…?" Keera balked.

"You deserve punishment," Diablo said, glaring at Keera, "and there is only one punishment fitting enough for having tried to kill me… Repent for your sins with death!"

"Eep!? S-Stop…!" His face terror-stricken, Keera backed away.

"At the very least, it will all be over in an instant."

Diablo pointed his staff at him.

"…Who… *What* are yooooou!?"

"I am a being born within a world of chaos, bound by no person— I am the Demon Lord, Diablo!"

"Ahhhhhh!" Keera turned tail and ran. "What… What the hell *is* this…? Why, why, why!? *Why* is something like that in front of me!? This can't be happening! It can't, it can't, it can't! Someone, quick! Someone save meeeeeeeeee!!"

— *Now he runs away?*

Diablo started opening his mouth…

—*Time to hit him with magic—*

"W-Wait!" A desperate shout rang out.

Shera clung to Diablo.

"Diablo, please! Let… Let my brother go."

—*After all the horrible things Keera did to her, I would think Shera wouldn't be able to forgive him…*

"You're not still in his control, are you?" Diablo asked for confirmation.

"No!"

"As master of the enslavement collar you bear, I command you: speak your true mind."

"I... I hate my brother... I really do. But, I don't want any more of my family to die. There were... times where we smiled and laughed together..."

Perhaps it was because he had forced it out of her using a command, but Shera's voice was shaking as she spoke. There could be no question about it: this was how Shera truly felt.

"Hmph..." Diablo lowered his staff. "There is no merit in killing an insect like him..."

"...Thank you, Diablo... and... I'm sorry." Shera cast her eyes downwards.

Diablo turned to look at Keera, who was disappearing deeper into the forest.

"It would certainly be a problem for me if you forgave him so easily."

As if objecting to Diablo's decision, the voice of a cool-headed, middle-aged man rang throughout the forest.

†

Diablo and the others could see it happening ten meters away from them—

As Keera tried to flee, a man in a white military uniform with a longsword strapped at his waist suddenly appeared in his way—

It was Galford.

From behind him, around twenty heavily armored foot soldiers quickly came into sight. It was completely unexpected— They must have been hiding using some kind of concealment spell.

Confused, Keera came to a halt.

"Y-You're the governor of Faltra!?"

"And you must be the prince of the Kingdom of Greenwood, though that detail is not even worth confirming. I have already seen everything."

Galford placed a hand on the hilt of his sword.

"Whoa, hey, whoa, whoa, whoa!?" Scared stiff, Keera backed away. "I'm the Elf prince, y-you know!? Do you know what's going to happen to you if you try and hurt me!?"

"There's something I would like to ask you as well: do you understand the meaning behind sending troops into another country's territory?"

"A-Are you trying to go to war with us!? You know, *war!?* A war between the Humans and Elves!?"

"The war had already started when *you* declared war on *us* and sent your soldiers in."

"No! That's not what I—"

"A difference of opinions. Quite the common occurrence when war breaks out."

Galford's figure wavered— The next moment, he was in front of Keera.

A sharp, metallic sound rang out as he sheathed his sword, seemingly without ever having taken it out.

Keera's head flew through the air.

Diablo doubted his own eyes—

Eyes open wide in horror, Shera screamed—

Rem covered her mouth, averting her eyes—

Alicia stared fixedly in shock—

Injured and unable to move, a commotion broke out from the Elves—

The Kingdom of Greenwood's prince had been effortlessly disposed of.

"What do you think you are doing?" Diablo stared menacingly at Galford.

Galford slowly walked forward. Wasting no time, he issued a command to his subordinates:

"Finish off the remaining Elf forces, but capture the princess alive. Eliminate anyone who gets in the way."

"You bastard... This was your plan all along!"

Diablo went to confront him. An unfazed expression on his face, Galford once again rested a hand on the hilt of his sword.

"If you plan on interfering, I will be forced to eliminate you as well."

As they glared at each other, Diablo spoke to the girls:

"Stay back, but don't get too far away. There may be soldiers approaching us from behind."

"What are you planning to do, Diablo?"

"It appears I'm going to have to talk some sense into him."

Rem and the others backed up about twenty meters away.

Galford turned his gaze towards Shera.

"Could you understand something for me? I have nothing I wish to speak with you about." He raised his left hand.

—*What is he trying to do!?*

At that moment, a flash of light shot through the forest.

—*Magic!*

The light surrounded itself around Diablo.

—*Another spell I don't know!? Damn, this has been happening too much lately!*

He tried to leave the area the light was covering—

With a high-pitched jolt, like the sound of static electricity, something had repelled Diablo's advance.

"Damn it, get out of my way! 《Explosion》!"

Facing Galford, Diablo launched the spell towards the governor. Rather than hitting his designated target, the area directly in front of Diablo exploded instead.

—*There's a wall here!?*

He couldn't see it, but he could feel some kind of barrier had enclosed around him.

"This is a ritual magic used to capture large-scale monsters," Galford said, stroking his chin. "For you, well, let's say it would be impossible for you to detect our preparations to use it. By yourself, you are indeed an exceptional Sorcerer... But we in the military excel at group combat."

"You bastard..."

"That barrier is able to seal even the most powerful of monsters. You won't be getting out of it so easily, so be good and stay put for a while."

—*Stuff like this exists as well!?*

Diablo had no idea what this kind of magic was. Since it prevented movement, it was close to "Bind" in that regard.

But Diablo was wearing equipment that rendered him invulnerable to negative status effects. If this could affect even him, then this was no ordinary effect— To begin with, if there was some kind of barrier in a game that could be activated in an instant and completely seal a player's movements, that would be a crappy game, no question.

For a solo player like Diablo, this completely shut him down. This aberrant feeling— It was like one of the cutscenes from the game.

Most of the time, in-game cutscenes made him want to yell, "Why the hell are you just standing there watching!?" Players had no control over what happened— It was all for the sake of the story. These were things like the Fallen gaining tremendous power, or an enormous monster getting resurrected, or some key NPC being abducted—and you just had to sit there and be a spectator to it all. If this were the game, then the only option would be to just watch it happen…

But being forced to watch a cutscene in real life wasn't something he could endure. In particular, the event Diablo was going to be forced to see would be particularly hard to stomach: the injured Elves would be slaughtered… Shera would be captured… And at worst, Rem and Alicia would be killed, too.

—*Screw that! I'm not gonna stand by and watch this crappy cutscene play out! Not while I can still do something!*

He placed his hands against the invisible wall.

—*I have to try dispelling this magic!*

The magic in Shera's enslavement collar was complicated, and far too complex—

But he knew the method needed to rid the invisible wall.

—*I have to make it work now!*

To be specific, he had to make contact with his hands and grasp the flow of magic energy. It was like unraveling a pile of tangled strings; if he rushed the process, things could get messy, and he would lose his grasp on the energy. He had to be careful while still going as fast as possible.

—*Hurry! Come on, hurry! Hurry!!*

Alicia stepped forward, passing Diablo and entering within striking distance of Galford.

"Governor, sir, I request an explanation for this!"

Galford cocked his head.

"This is the duty of the governor of Faltra: crush any invaders, and protect the races."

"Are you planning to invade Greenwood as well!?"

"It seems you suffer from a misunderstanding here. Mobilizing an army within my own territory cannot be called an invasion. This is merely self-defense."

"Ngh… But why would go and kill an opponent who has already surrendered!?"

"Surrendered? These Elves? It does not appear that way to me—"

"Furthermore, is it necessary to abduct the princess!?"

"She was almost taken away after I left the task to these 'Adventurers.' I have deemed it necessary that the army should now take custody of her. Is an Imperial Knight trying to interfere with how the military conducts itself?"

"There is nothing humane about your actions! Withdraw your troops immediately, and release Sir Diablo!"

"Return to the Royal Capital and make whatever report you like. The Kingdom of Greenwood, however, may have already surrendered by then."

"Then… I will stop you!" Alicia drew her sword.

"And how, exactly, do you intend to stop me using a sword without a blade?" Galford asked, bemused.

"H-Huh?" Perplexed, Alicia looked down at her sword. It was obvious something about its weight was different than usual.

Without a sound, the sword had broken, its blade falling to the ground.

"Wha—!?"

Sweat broke out along Alicia's brow; Diablo shuddered as well.

—*He cut through Alicia's sword!?*

Diablo had just barely managed to see what Galford's mirage had done: the instant Alicia drew her sword, Galford had sliced clean through it.

—*He's on a completely different level than any Adventurer or soldier...*

From what Diablo could tell, Galford was over level 100. He was already beyond the limits of any of the races. At this rate, Diablo wouldn't know how strong he really was without actually confronting him directly.

The max level in-game was 150, but after all the other unimplemented gameplay elements Diablo had seen in this world, he couldn't afford to let his guard down. At worst, Diablo had to consider the possibility that Galford was stronger than himself.

"Alicia." Galford shook his head. "It seems you are not suited for combat after all. Return to the Royal Capital and tell them whatever you like. I'm sure His Majesty will listen to whomever is stronger. The city of Faltra is the front line in case of a Fallen invasion, after all."

"Ngh..." Alicia collapsed to her knees.

Faced with an overwhelming difference in their power, it was only natural she would lose her will to fight. The same thing had happened to the Elves Diablo had fought against.

Galford thrust his left hand forwards.

"Commence the operation— All troops, move out! Capture the princess, and eliminate anyone who interferes!"

Galford's heavily armored troops let out a battle cry. The Elves screamed in terror, injured and unable to run away.

"Stop it!!" Shera cried out.

Rem readied her metal claws.

"...It doesn't seem he will stop just because you ask him to."

True, Galford probably wouldn't be stopped by mere words; but the fact Alicia had bought them even the slightest amount of time was not in vain.

"Heh heh heh... You say the King will listen to who is stronger? Then my words will be absolute, Galford."

"Silence. I will be dealing with you later. I also have a ritual magic prepared for just—"

In one deft movement, Diablo pulled at the end of the magical energy. The threads of magic that made up the barrier started to come undone, just like he had untied the ribbon on a present.

Then, with a sharp, high-pitched sound of something breaking, the barrier came crumbling down.

†

"Impossible..." Galford's eyes narrowed. "He broke through the barrier...!? All units— Halt!"

Receiving the order, the soldiers on the verge of attacking the Elves about-faced, scrambling to make their way back behind Galford.

Diablo flashed a fearless smile.

"You are a fool to think something like that could hold me!"

—Although I was cutting it pretty dang close!

Thank goodness I did a practice run with Shera… Though, it was kinda embarrassing, thinking back to it…

Diablo faced Galford, who stood about ten meters away from him. Alicia was still on the ground between them, so he couldn't just rush in with a huge AoE spell right from the start.

Galford unsheathed his sword.

"Hm… I should have dealt with you first. I had considered the possibility of the Elves and the princess running off while I did so, however…"

"From the very beginning, you were planning to pit the Elves against me so we would wear each other out, all so you could come in and finish us off."

"That is called 'strategy,' though I suppose an Adventurer like you wouldn't know of such things."

"Hmph— A coward's method."

—This is why I hate those wargamers…

"Being scorned by one's enemies is the greatest praise for a soldier."

"I will deliver unto you the ultimate despair. You will never be able to scorn *anyone* when I am through with you! Explosion!"

Diablo set off another explosion, just barely missing Alicia still crouched on the ground. She might be on the receiving end of some of the fallout from the blast, but she would just have to grit her teeth and bear it.

Galford had leapt back so fast, it seemed he had disappeared entirely.

—He dodged my spell!? Diablo hadn't thought it possible.

—Players with high speed stats were able to "resist" certain things in-game, but is that the reason here?

Galford instantly closed the gap between them. It was fast, but Diablo saw it—

A rapid thrust.

Diablo turned his body to the side to avoid the attack. As if he had already read Diablo's movements, Galford changed the trajectory of his sword—

A sideways slash, gashing Diablo's arm.

He was taking even more damage.

—He's breaking through my damage-reducing abilities like they're nothing!

The damage he took, however, still wasn't as bad as when he took Edelgard's 《Sacrificial Charge》 during their fight. These were normal attacks, not Martial Arts, after all.

Galford kept up his attacks: a thrust; sideways slice; a swipe at Diablo's legs; an upwards rising slash.

He's insanely fast!

Usually, Diablo would try to back away, putting some distance between him and the enemy. That was the basic strategy for any Sorcerer vs. Warrior fight; but he held his ground. It wouldn't seem very cool for a Demon Lord to fight while running away— However, this wasn't the only reason he stood firm:

Rem and Shera were behind him, about twenty meters away. If he tried to back off they would immediately be caught up in the fight.

—I can't just blindly move backwards here...

Staying within range of Galford's sword put him at an overwhelming disadvantage as he kept receiving more and more damage from Galford's sword.

His wounds hurt; he was most likely bleeding; but because of his high HP, he still had health to spare...

But at this rate, it was only a matter of time for him. To make matters worse, there was another reason he couldn't simply back up and launch a counteroffensive—

As if he had read his mind, Galford spoke:

"You seem to be considerably worn out after taking on those Elves earlier. For a Sorcerer who supposedly fended off an army of Fallen, your movements are quite sluggish, aren't they?"

Even whilst talking, Galford never let up on his attacks.

—*Even after swinging his sword around that much, he isn't breathing hard or anything. Frankly, that's amazing... But, wait— I guess I should think of it more as him dedicating himself to the whole,* "Focus on not letting up on your attacks when facing a Sorcerer, rather than the strength behind each strike" *strategy. It looks like he's a master of one-on-one combat, too.*

"Hmph..." Diablo's face turned into a twisted smile. "You're just so weak that I can't work up the motivation to actually try!"

A bluff— This was the most damage he had ever received.

"How about putting some distance between us and using your magic?" Galford scoffed.

—*He's seen through me after all...*

Rem, Shera, and Alicia were still about twenty meters away. He couldn't back up and let them get involved, and Galford knew this well.

—*I have to stop him here.*

—*No, that's impossible. I can't win if I'm within reach of that sword.*

Diablo took a giant leap backwards, with Galford pursuing him.

"As I thought, you value your own life over theirs!"

He was closing in fast. Moving into close-quarters was the most basic of basics for a Warrior when fighting against a Sorcerer.

"Your movements are deft, that much is for sure. However! That only makes it all the easier to predict your next move, Galford!"

As Diablo fell back, he cast a spell under his breath. For the moment, it seemed like nothing had happened...

Galford made his approach—and the ground exploded at his feet.

"What!?"

—*My magic must have completely taken him by surprise.*

The attack— 《Super Mine》, a spell that could be placed and used as a trap. It would activate upon whatever part of the ground the caster aimed at, and would deal damage to anyone who passed over it. Diablo had used an advanced version of the spell, one that could be acquired around level 80. Despite the level it was learned at, it didn't deal much damage; but it activated quickly. It was a spell perfectly suited for dealing with opponents who would move in close to fight.

—*Looks like I managed to wound his leg.*

But it wasn't enough to stop the governor from moving. Diablo kept laying down more "Super Mines"; but even after seeing it only the once, Galford had discerned it to be a spell that exploded when passed over. His perception was impressive, to say the least.

Moving forwards in a dizzying zigzag pattern, Galford made his approach; an appropriate strategy in response to the mines.

"It's been thirty years since someone has successfully wounded me, Diablo!"

"Is that so... Then not having more opponents capable of doing the same will be your downfall, Galford! The steps people take to get closer to Sorcerers in combat, and the magic needed to guard against it— You will never know the endless hours I have spent researching just for this moment! Such is the world I come from!!"

—*He still has much to learn.*

Galford was almost superhuman. Never mind the other races in this world: he was liable to have some of the most powerful stats in the game as well.

But the one standing before him was no ordinary player—

Diablo, the Demon Lord, a being so powerful that he slaughtered countless challengers who had come to face him.

He had never lost when it came to predicting his opponent's moves. A "Super Mine" exploded underneath Galford's feet, stalling his movement.

—*There's my chance.*

Diablo pointed his staff at Galford, casting a spell:

"Turn to frost: 《Freeze Zone》!"

This was a level 90 Ice-elemental spell that would freeze a small targeted area. Though it wouldn't outright defeat an opponent, it would apply the 《Freeze》 status effect to them, slowing their movement.

With a resounding crackle, Galford, the ground surrounding him, and the air itself was flash frozen.

—*Got you.*

Diablo promptly pumped his fist, then quickly regained his composure.

—*Is he gonna be all right? That was a pretty strong spell.*

∴Crap, I might have killed him.

The ice crumbled away. For a split-second, Diablo was worried about his opponent's well-being—

Galford rushed towards him, completely unharmed.

—*It didn't work at all!?*

Impossible…

If that's the case, then it must be a Martial Art that provides him with absolute defense!

The timing for it was strict, but there was a Martial Art in the game that allowed you to completely negate one attack from your opponent in battle. It almost seemed like cheating to use it, but that's what you could expect from someone over level 100.

Galford grandly swung his sword overhead.

—He's gonna unleash a big one!

Diablo was completely defenseless. No matter how short the spell, there was always a period of time you couldn't move after using magic.

Galford must have decided he was going to end their fight right now; his sword started to glow red-hot as heat enveloped the blade.

—《Heat Sonic》.

A Martial Art that could be learned at level 120, it was a technique that turned the user's blade red-hot. This allowed the wielder to unleash a series of eight slashes almost instantaneously.

—Was the "chance" I got from my "Super Mine" just an act to entice me into using an even bigger spell? Then he'd use his technique to completely guard against my magic and hit me with his finishing move…

Everyone thinks the same thing.

"A Demon Lord has no blind spots!"

"What are you saying now!?"

The blade of the sword was drawing closer. Keeping himself exposed to this danger, Diablo shouted:

"The reason you will lose is that you have only fought weaklings your whole life! 《Omit》— 《Lightning Bullet》!!"

"Whaaaaat!?"

Just as the name would suggest, "Omit" was a special skill that allowed the user to skip the casting time for a spell. It was similar to a Warrior's Martial Art moreso than actual magic.

Lightning Bullet was classified as an advanced Light-elemental spell. This caused bullets of light to speed towards the rapidly approaching Galford. He had already committed to using his Martial Art, so there was nothing he could do in response.

The bullets bore into his chest, and sent him flying backwards. A dull heft of breath escaped his lungs as he crashed into the hard ground, tearing up the terrain itself as he scraped along it.

The bullets of light swiftly burst, dealing even heavier damage to him.

Galford was covered in burns from the attack, his white uniform in tatters. Black smoke was rising from his body. Yet even then, he was still on one knee, using his sword as a cane to raise himself up.

Diablo was impressed.

—*Phew, that's just the kind of HP I'd expect out of him! Glad he's not dead...*

It was true Galford had murdered Keera, but Diablo did not want to kill anyone he didn't absolutely have to.

"What happened to the 'finishing blow'?" Galford said with a grunt of pain. "I'm still alive, you know..."

"Hmph... This battle is over. I am no longer interested in you."

Diablo gave a derisive snort, but on the inside, a wave of relief washed over him.

—*But that was still pretty dangerous!*

In the end, the reason he won was thanks to his experience fighting against other people, as well as the difference in their skill expertise. Yet, Galford had easily been the strongest enemy he had faced since coming to this world.

—But I can't let him think he almost had me— He might just come after me again. I won, so I might as well threaten him a little.

"You were much more of a weakling than I expected. You disappoint me! Know that you are not even remotely a match for me!" Diablo spoke as arrogantly as possible.

"…Are you saying you don't plan to kill me?" Galford scowled.

"If you wish to die, then do as you please."

"Are you sure about that? I may just deliver a report to the King that makes things much, much worse for you."

—That… actually might be kinda bad.

"I will not allow that to happen." Right then, Alicia walked over to them, having recovered from her previous stupor. "I will prepare my own report to the King, one that states how you fully intended to sabotage the harmony between Faltra and its neighboring country!"

"…And?" Galford scoffed. "Between the governor of Faltra and a single Imperial Knight— Whose report do you think he will believe?"

"His Majesty is a person of great intelligence and wisdom."

"I would think it more efficient to kill me right here."

—If he's going that far, then it makes me think this is some kind of trap… He seems like he'd come back to haunt me if I killed him, too.

Diablo was troubled. This was the first time an opponent he had claimed victory over had made him feel so… uncomfortable.

Even so, going back on what he had said would make him seem lame.

"Hmph… Pointless. As I've said, if you wish to die, then do as you like. If you wish to challenge me again, then I will gladly be your opponent. But the next time you think of raising a hand against me or one of my possessions— Know that I will reduce you and the land you govern to cinders!"

He was a little iffy about threatening the town itself, but he still said it anyways, just in case. Diablo wanted to ensure no one would go after Rem and Shera, after all.

Galford stood back up.

—*He wants to go another round!? Right* now!? *Noooo!*

"You say all that, and yet you will not take my life…" Galford breathed a sigh. "Is this just on a whim? Or is this part of some grand scheme of yours?"

—*I just want to save as many lives as I can…*

But that wasn't very Demon Lord-like at all, so he would never say that out loud, of course.

"Hmph… I simply feel like it."

"You might come to regret not killing me."

"If you dare face me again, *you* shall be the one to regret having survived here."

Galford turned his back to him. Then, raising his left hand—

"All troops, fall back!"

His voice resonated throughout the battlefield. The soldiers who had been watching the battle sprinted over, lining up in front of Galford. As the sound of their marching reverberated over the terrain, they made their retreat.

Diablo stared at Galford's back as he left.

—*So, it's finally over…*

He had no idea what was going to happen from here on out… For now, he had managed to put an end to the fight before him.

—*It may have not been the best outcome, but I think I can call it the* second *best conclusion to all of this.*

Diablo turned his gaze towards Rem and Shera.

†

Rem ran towards him.

"Are you all right!?"

"No problems whatsoever." Diablo nodded. "I was only toying with him, after all."

"…For you to win against Galford, even after having fought those other battles beforehand… You truly are amazing."

Diablo was happy enough that he wanted to do a little victory dance—but instead gave a reserved sneer more fitting of a Demon Lord.

"But of course."

Diablo saw Shera run over to Keera's dead body. He was also planning on going over there as well, but…

—I'm so wiped out that even walking is a pain…

He just wanted to fall asleep where he stood.

"Um… Do you have any potions to spare…?" Rem asked Diablo.

"Hm? Were you hurt?"

"No, it's not that… I want to use it on the Elves."

—It's true, we'd probably be able to save a lot of them with potions.

Diablo took the HP potions he had made this morning from his pouch.

—But it's not cool for a Demon Lord to use his own items to save someone else…

"Well uh, you see… I have some things I wanted to run a few experiments with. These potions are too weak to have any effect on me, so… Go see if we can actually put these to use."

He gave Rem the potion flasks.

"…You really are kind after all."

"F-Fool!" Diablo shouted to hide his embarrassment. "Keep saying foolish things like that and I'll destroy this whole forest!"

"...I don't think I would be able to survive that, so I think I'll go tend to the Elves now." Rem smiled.

—She's seen right through me... I guess there's no getting around that after we've spent all this time together.

Diablo sighed.

"Hurry up and go, before I change my mind."

"...All right. I leave Shera to you." She ran off towards the injured Elves.

—That's right: I have to go see Shera.

Next, Alicia came to speak with him:

"Sir Galford is sure to make a nonbeneficial report towards you... Are you sure you are all right with this?" The expression on her face was serious.

—Are you telling me to kill him? Although, I guess her working as a knight in this world means she has a different sense for these kinds of situations than I do.

Even so, it's kind of hard to call Galford the "bad guy" here— After all, this whole thing was caused by Keera's violent recklessness.

I still think Galford's actions were cruel and heavy-handed, though. I can't say for certain if it was actually necessary to kill Keera.

But Galford hadn't been acting for personal gain; rather, it was to protect this country. Since Galford had been the one to challenge Diablo, all he had done was thrash the governor in response to that. He had no intention of judging who was good or evil; and he wasn't a god either, nor did he have the privileges or obligations of one. In the end, both Galford and the Elves had their reasons for doing this, but both were also to blame here.

—I'm really not a fan of war after all.

Diablo already had enough of going through the trouble of fighting off armies. If he showed weakness now, someone could end up taking advantage of that.

"I am no god, nor am I an enforcer of the law; I am a Demon Lord," Diablo informed Alicia. "I will kill whomever I please, and spare who I want. If the king chooses to believe Galford's words over your own and dares to oppose me, then I will butcher this entire country."

It was half a threat, half the truth. If Galford had used his soldiers during their battle, then it would have been impossible for Diablo to fight without killing anyone. Since he didn't have that much MP remaining, it would have been more efficient for him to blast everyone with an AoE spell rather than disabling each soldier one-by-one.

Now, if the king truly did send the national armies to oppose Diablo, his only choice would be to fight with the intent of killing them all.

—If I really do want peace, the best thing would be to not resist, I guess.

So, in that case, if I don't kill anyone, then I get killed instead...

He was no saint. If such a situation really did come to pass, he wouldn't be satisfied with dying a pacifist's death.

"I understand your intentions." Alicia nodded. "This time, *I* shall be the one to try and prevent a war from occurring between you and Lyferia."

"Do as you wish."

—I'm counting on you! Pretty please!!

Suddenly, Alicia turned her gaze towards Rem. Diablo followed suit.

Rem was working in earnest, calling out to see if any of the Elves were seriously injured.

Alicia let out a sigh of admiration.

"To be honest, I would imagine she's exhausted... It seems she does not have a drop of MP left, either."

"Hm... Rem did end up calling forth her Summons, after all."

"She looks almost angelic, doesn't she..." Alicia faintly muttered under her breath.

—*I feel like I just heard her ask if this is having an effect on Rem's personality...*

But what does she mean? Is it really that strange for an Adventurer to help other people when there's no money involved for them?

Maybe he had heard her wrong— Putting it bluntly, he had lost so much HP and MP that he would fall asleep on the spot if he let his concentration slip for so much as a second. He had probably misheard her because of that.

—*Not good! Falling asleep standing up like a salaryman taking the last train home is* not *Demon Lord-like!*

He tried to boost his spirits with some Demon Lord role play:

"Hmph! Every one of my opponents has left me unsatisfied. Is there anyone in this country that will make me use my true power!?"

He held his staff aloft as Alicia stared intently at him.

"You are certainly a being to be feared, Sir Diablo... You might even be a true Demon Lord..."

Strangely enough, he felt a kind of affection from her... No, it was something even more than that. One might even call it adoration.

—*I thought she'd be a little more freaked out about this. Even though I've fought all these battles, maybe she sees through me too, since I have yet to actually kill anyone...*

"I *am* a Demon Lord. Have you not listened to what I've said?"

"Yes, please forgive me… Sir Diablo, please, go over to be with Miss Shera soon."

"Will you not accompany me?"

"I will go help Miss Rem. I believe it would be best for Miss Shera if it were just the two of you." With an enigmatic smile, Alicia walked back towards Rem.

—*Maybe it's just something only girls would understand…?*

Shera was motionless in the middle of the forest. Her shoulders drooped as she stood in front of her brother's unmoving corpse.

They hadn't been able to save him.

Diablo had tried to speak— But there were no words his Demon Lord act could provide to comfort someone who had just lost a family member.

Shera wiped her tears. Having noticed Diablo approaching, she turned to look at him for only an instant.

He had to say something, so he opened his mouth:

"…Um…"

"Yeah…"

With just that short conversation, they became silent once again. But before long, Shera started to talk, eyes still cast downwards.

"…There wasn't any way to avoid this, huh… I don't know much about how both countries got along, but I know my brother did a bad thing."

Her voice was shaking. Though it was obvious she was only trying to act strong, she wouldn't say how she really felt.

In the end, Diablo couldn't say anything. He couldn't fully express how he felt with words.

He laid a hand on her shoulder. Shera looked up at him, her eyes blurred with an endless stream of tears pouring down her white cheeks.

She buried herself in Diablo's arms and cried her heart out.

There were no words; rather, the tears themselves proclaimed how she truly felt.

It didn't matter what the deceased had done or what their personality was— Losing family was sad, and anyone would feel the same.

Diablo stroked Shera's golden hair. He had a feeling it would be best to stay like this until Shera had calmed down.

†

After returning from the Eastern Lakefront Forest—

Alicia immediately left on a trip to the Royal Capital, apparently to make a report of this incident directly to the king. Diablo had wanted to escort her himself, since the governor's troops might go after Alicia to prevent her from making an unfavorable report to the king about the governor…

The name of the Demon Lord Diablo had spread farther than he had expected, so Diablo's arrival could end up being a cause for alarm for the king, so she had turned down his offer. With this last incident, the stakes had been raised even higher, according to Alicia. So far, he had silenced an elite squadron of Elves; obliterated a towering Summon; and above all else, emerged victorious in a battle against the hero Galford. If someone as otherworldly-powerful as him were to approach the Royal Capital unannounced, it wouldn't be strange for the king to overreact in that situation.

Diablo was basically a one-man army. If a country they had no diplomatic relationships with suddenly marched on the Royal Capital, this could only be called one thing: "invasion"— There was no room for doubt on that.

That was the reason behind Alicia's refusal to Diablo's offer of escort.

—I probably don't need to worry about her; Alicia is plenty strong. She may not have been a match for Galford, but she played an active role in our fight against the Elves.

And she did say the king "would surely resolve this matter peacefully" before rushing off. Let's just hope she brings back good news.

Peace is best, after all.

It had been three days since the battle with the Elves, and Diablo was lying down in the bed at the inn after once again almost using all his MP. He was, once more, spending his days not doing anything, waiting for it to recover.

Galford hadn't made any kind of move yet, but he could attack at any time. Diablo wanted to recover his MP as fast as possible, but the MP potions he had in his pouch when he was first summoned to this world were particularly potent. He didn't want to use them unless it was an absolute emergency.

That being said, however, he couldn't get hold of the materials necessary to make MP potions, so he didn't have the chance to put his Combiner skills to work.

—But people are always growing.

He wasn't going to spend another ten days in a row lazing around like last time. He had put in a request with Sylvie to bring him an MP potion. Being the Guildmaster, she should at the very least be able to gather up the ingredients he needed. This was his third day waiting for a response, though…

He was on his own today as Rem and Shera had headed out on an errand after taking on an easy quest. But he should have gone with them— He was worried about what Galford would do now.

—But, my motivation… And my MP…

Not being able to do the things he wanted was the very definition of running out of MP. It was like spending your time doing stupid things when you should have been studying for exams; or playing games when you have a deadline right around the corner.

According to Rem, Galford wouldn't try to make anyone his enemy if they were stronger than himself, not if he didn't have to. The governor's ultimate priority was to protect the city of Faltra; given the present situation, even a child could understand that having Diablo as an ally would be a boon for the city.

Since Shera was an Elven princess, he was also worried about her being taken as a hostage… But Shera herself had laughed it off, saying that, even if he would get the princess of a small country for doing it, making Diablo an enemy after demonstrating how strong he was would be a complete loss for Galford.

If Diablo took away the girls' freedom because of how worried he was, then he would just be doing the same thing as Keera. "An Adventurer should be able to protect themselves!" This was one of the basic principles of the job.

In any case, Galford shouldn't make any moves until the king made a decision after hearing Alicia's report. As for the Kingdom of Greenwood, Celsior said he would report everything that had happened. He had also said Shera shouldn't have to worry about being chased after any longer.

The reason they had been trying to bring her back in the first place was because of Keera's own judgment. Apparently, Shera's father had been half-hearted about forcibly making her return. Of course, Shera's bounty had disappeared as well. He didn't know how Greenwood would react to Keera's death yet, though.

Putting all that aside— He had been forced to come face to face with something truly horrible.

There was no reward for their last quest—

And there was no reward for avoiding the war.

I'm gonna freakin' murder you, Galford!!

—Agh, I lost some MP because I was so angry just now. Right when I was getting it back…

Diablo stopped and took a deep breath. This had been a request from the governor to prevent a war between the Elves and Faltra, after all.

—I ended up fighting the guy who gave us the quest, so I guess I should have seen this coming.

Even if he hadn't been a Demon Lord, anyone asking for a reward the day after beating the crap out of their client was just impossible. Essentially, he had ended up working for free the past few days.

Buying his war scythe and ingredients for potions had put him in the red. The result: Diablo, now out of MP, had reverted to being a NEET, with Rem and Shera were taking on things like "gathering quests" for the rewards.

—This is a leecher's lifestyle! I'm the worst…

Suddenly, loud knocking came from the door. Collecting himself, Diablo answered:

"Enter as you like."

The door opened with a creak. A small girl entered, wearing her usual outfit that made her look half-naked—

It was Sylvie.

"Hi there, Diablo! How are you? Not well, huh. Right."

"Yeah."

"Well, I've got some good news for you today."

"Oh hoh? Did you manage to bring what I asked for?"

"Nooooot exactly... But hey, it should do just about the same thing." Sylvie took out what she was hiding behind her back.

—Is that a bottle of booze?

He couldn't read the words on it, but he was pretty sure that's what it was.

"So, it's *not* an MP potion?"

"It's actually a kind of alcohol that has a similar effect to one. Because potions are effective even in small doses, they're pretty expensive and rare. But this is so much easier to find, and it tastes good to boot! It's some pretty strong stuff, but I bet you should be all right with it, Diablo."

"This will recover my MP, then?"

"Yup, that's for sure! How effective it is seems to vary, though. Ah, I brought some cheese, too."

—Strong stuff, huh.

He didn't know exactly *how* strong it was, but Diablo's body was tough. He also had the skill that neutralized negative status effects, so it was possible he wouldn't even get tipsy.

—There was never a 《Drunk》 status effect back in Cross Reverie, though that may not matter right now. I'll just have to give it a try.

"Then I will take it." Diablo nodded. Sitting on the edge of the bed, he extended his hand.

Sylvie pulled the cork from the bottle; a fruity aroma spread throughout the room. Judging from the powerful smell of grapes, it seemed to be some kind of wine.

She handed it over to him, where he drank the whole thing in one gulp.

"Ohh!" Sylvie clapped her hands. "Just as I thought; you sure can handle your liquor!"

"…Ahh… Of courshe! I am… a Deeemon Lord!"

"Um… You *can* handle it…right?"

Diablo's body started to get warm; he was feeling pretty good. His vision started to swim— Unable to even keep himself sitting upright, he fell back on the bed.

In a panic, Sylvie ran over to him.

"Hey, hold on! Are you all right, Diablo!?"

—It's like I'm underwater…

Everything sounded so far away as his surroundings twisted and turned.

—It's so hot. I need something cold…

As he thought that, he blindly reached out with wandering hands—

—managing to grab on to something; something slender and soft. It was cool to the touch, just perfect for him now. With a tug, he pulled it towards himself.

"Wh-What is it, Diablo!?"

For a moment, Diablo hallucinated himself back in his own bed in the real world.

—Man, I'm so sleepy… Sleepy… Oh? There's a body pillow here.

"Mm…" Without being completely aware of it himself, he had dragged Sylvie onto the bed.

"Waaaah!?"

"Mm… This is the stuff…" He embraced her.

"Diablo!? This is kind of making me uncomfortable!!"

"Mmm… So comfy to hug… Just what I want from a good body pillow. I'd take out a loan just to buy this…"

"What's a body pillow!? And what do you mean by 'taking out a loan'!?"

"Hmm? There's something on it… Something in the way of the smooth feeling…"

"W-Wait! You can't pull that! This is bad, Diablo! E-Even I'd get mad if you went any further than this!"

"It's so smooth…"

"Nnngh! You're supposed to be a Sorcerer— How are you this strong…!?"

Half asleep, Diablo started to stroke her. Sylvie twisted in his arms.

"Ahn! No! You can't touch there! I'm a Grasswalker, and you're a Demon, so us doing this is— Doing this is…! It isn't right! Ah! Ahn! Not there! You can't go down from there, Diablo! Ahhhhhnn!"

Shuddering, Sylvie's back arched like a bow.

"…Hah… Hah… G-Geez, Diablo… Are you planning on taking responsibility for this…? Hm? Huh?"

"Zzz…mrgh…mumble…"

"…He's asleep!?"

Sylvie struggled to break free from Diablo's arms. Even though he was sound asleep, however, Diablo's arms would not be moved so easily.

"At least let go of me before you sleep! Rem and Shera are gonna come back soon!! —And give me back my clothes!"

A pool of blood spread from the corpse of a knight lying on the ground. The emblem on his armor proved he belonged to the city of Faltra's military.

The middle of the forest—

It was a place hidden inside thickets of trees, hindering anyone from seeing it on the outside.

Alicia flicked her sword; splatters of blood and fat flew off it. The corpse of a knight laid at her feet.

"Unsightly…" Alicia spat the word at the dead knight. "Why is it that, alive or dead, the races are just so… unsightly…"

A lone girl stood in front of Alicia, her silver hair coming down to her waist. She had dark-colored skin and large, youthful, golden eyes. Her pupils were vertical slits, just like that of a reptile. She wasn't part of the races from this world—

She was a Fallen. Her name:

Edelgard.

"You saying that… strange, I think," she muttered. "Alicia is one of the races, too, yes?"

She almost sounded like she was sulking.

"I think of myself as unsightly as well, Lady Edelgard. I am not as beautiful as you are." Alicia gave a self-deriding smile.

"But now, Fallen are weak?" Edelgard tilted her head.

"Surely you jest! Your kind are far more proficient and beautiful than any of the races! You are anything but weak!"

"Still, not enough. Since Lord Enkvaros fell... Fallen, and monsters? Weak. No more, being born. Losing more, all the time."

"Yes, I am aware of that... The Demon Lord of the Mind, Enkvaros, was said to hold the power of 'Magic Reflection'— I may know someone who comes close to that description."

Diablo was the one who came to Alicia's mind; he called himself a Demon Lord. From what she had heard, he was able to reflect all magic. Alicia never had a chance to see for herself, but there was no doubt about his power. He almost perfectly fit the rumors she had heard of the Demon Lord.

"But, he makes allies, with other races? Edelgard tilted her head.

—*Now that I think about it, Lady Edelgard and Sir Diablo have met before, haven't they.*

"Yes, unfortunately..." she nodded. "He always seems to avoid killing them."

"That's, why... I think Demon Lord, may be in, different place?"

Just as Edelgard said, Alicia had considered the possibility that Diablo was not the Demon Lord they sought, and there was another "true" Demon Lord to be found somewhere else. The Fallen were able to feel the presence of this Demon Lord if they could touch skin. It was possible they would be able to tell if Diablo was a genuine Demon Lord if they could make contact with him.

It was something impossible for Alicia to do.

—*How unsightly... The races truly are inferior.*

She decided to get into the issue at hand.

"Regarding that, I was unable to pry further about Sir Diablo because he never lets his guard down... However, I did try investigating Rem, the Pantherian girl who stays at his side. The beauty of the soul inside of her... It moved me deeply."

"...Demon Lord?" The look in Edelgard's eyes sharpened.

Alicia tilted her head, troubled.

"How accurate is the 《Identification Magic》 you taught me?"

"...Like, a magic trick? Know *how* it works, you will know *if* it worked. If you don't, then kind of unclear?"

"Then, unfortunately, I cannot say for certain. However, the soul trapped inside of Rem could very well be that of the Demon Lord."

As if copying Alicia, Edelgard tilted her head as well.

"Plan? Kill her?"

"Will the Demon Lord be revived if she dies?"

"Mm... Don't know. Will try it."

"Would it not be a problem if we lost the soul because of that? Even then, she has Sir Diablo by her side as well. What shall we do about this?"

"Leave to you."

"Hehe... Once I return to Faltra, I shall endeavor to live up to the trust you have placed in me. As for now, I must head to the Royal Capital to deliver my report stating that all is normal here; so there will be no interference from any of their Imperial Knights or military."

"Give you lift, to Royal Capital?"

Edelgard looked towards the deeper part of the forest. There, her most trusted mount and a type of Fallen—a 《Grand Dragon》—laid in wait.

"No." Alicia shook her head. "I would come under suspicion if I were to move too fast."

"Mm… Then, Edelgard ask Fallen priests, about other ways for Demon Lord's resurrection."

"Sir Diablo is extremely powerful… Please take care not to let him sense your presence."

"I know." She sounded a bit sulky.

Their conversation finished, Edelgard made her exit. Alicia stared at her as she left, spellbound.

—*Beautiful…*

Such a beautiful existence. This world should be ruled over by these beautiful Fallen— These unsightly races should all just disappear.

That's all Alicia ever wished for.

To be continued…

Thank you for reading the second volume of *How NOT to Summon a Demon Lord*!

I'm the author, Yukiya Murasaki.

We received an almost shocking amount of positive feedback after the release of volume one, so thank you very much for that! Before this volume has even released, it's been decided that this series is getting a manga! I never thought that I would get to talk about it this soon. It's all thanks to your support.

Naoto Fukuda is the artist for the manga. It will start being posted sometime in June through "Wednesday Serious" on Nico Nico Web Manga (free to read the latest chapters).

In this volume, we saw Diablo and the others do battle with Greenwood—or should I say, Prince Keera—after they sent in their elite Elf soldiers. Diablo managed to both recover the princess AND fight off Galford, happy to have lived up to his name as the Demon Lord—though we know that's just role play, and on the inside, he's still as nervous as ever.

The last volume was mostly about magic, so this time I tried focusing more on things like shopping and potion-making. I also delved a bit deeper into the characters and the lore of the world.

In the next volume, we have some sudden developments in the works! As Edelgard and the other Fallen close in on Rem, the Demon

Lord Krebskulm will finally be resurrected… maybe. I'm hoping it will be released sometime during the summer.

Special thanks—

Takahiro Tsurusaki, the illustrator, has been with me since we discussed where the plot should go. Thank you once again for the wonderfully bold and daring illustrations. They were amazing. *Very* amazing.

Thank you once again to Ooishi, the designer from Afterglow. The balance of the cover was just superb.

Thank you to my editor, Shouji, for being my emotional support and telling me, "This was another fun volume!"

Thanks to all the staff at the Kodansha Light Novel Editing Department, and to the family and friends who supported me.

And for all of you who have read this, I can only offer you my utmost gratitude. Thank you all very much!

Yukiya Murasaki

VOLUME 3
ON SALE
APRIL 2019!

How NOT to Summon a Demon Lord

Yukiya Murasaki

Illust. Takahiro Tsurusaki

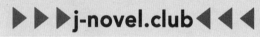

VOLUMES 1-2
ON SALE
FEBRUARY 2019!

In Another World With My Smartphone

©Patora Fuyuhara, Illustration: Eiji Usatsuka

J-Novel Club Lineup

Ebook Releases Series List

Amagi Brilliant Park
An Archdemon's Dilemma: How to Love Your Elf Bride
Ao Oni
Arifureta Zero
Arifureta: From Commonplace to World's Strongest
Bluesteel Blasphemer
Brave Chronicle: The Ruinmaker
Clockwork Planet
Demon King Daimaou
Der Werwolf: The Annals of Veight
ECHO
From Truant to Anime Screenwriter: My Path to "Anohana" and "The Anthem of the Heart"
Gear Drive
Grimgar of Fantasy and Ash
How a Realist Hero Rebuilt the Kingdom
How NOT to Summon a Demon Lord
I Saved Too Many Girls and Caused the Apocalypse
If It's for My Daughter, I'd Even Defeat a Demon Lord
In Another World With My Smartphone
Infinite Dendrogram
Infinite Stratos
Invaders of the Rokujouma!?
JK Haru is a Sex Worker in Another World
Kokoro Connect
Last and First Idol
Lazy Dungeon Master
Me, a Genius? I Was Reborn into Another World and I Think They've Got the Wrong Idea!
Mixed Bathing in Another Dimension
My Big Sister Lives in a Fantasy World
My Little Sister Can Read Kanji
My Next Life as a Villainess: All Routes Lead to Doom!
Occultic;Nine
Outbreak Company
Paying to Win in a VRMMO
Seirei Gensouki: Spirit Chronicles
Sorcerous Stabber Orphen: The Wayward Journey
The Faraway Paladin
The Magic in this Other World is Too Far Behind!
The Master of Ragnarok & Blesser of Einherjar
The Unwanted Undead Adventurer
Walking My Second Path in Life
Yume Nikki: I Am Not in Your Dream